UNEX
MIRACLES

Powerful real-life stories

ALISS CRESSWELL

Unexpected Miracles

All Scripture quotations are taken from the New International Version © 1973, 1978, 1984, 2011 by International Bible Society unless otherwise stated.

Photo credit page 142: Chris Furlong, Getty Images.

ISBN 13: 9780957264267
ISBN 10: 0957264267

Published by FiftyFive Eleven Ltd

Printed in the USA

More information and resources:
www.SpiritLifestyle.com

ABOUT THE AUTHOR

Aliss Cresswell believes in the God of miracles and living a life full of love and power. After giving up her dream home and her career to pioneer 'miracle' cafés and shops in England, Aliss along with her husband Rob, now inspire people all over the world to encounter God for themselves. Through their writing, speaking, videos and supernatural events, they train those who pursue a Spirit-filled life to demonstrate God's power and release miracles everywhere they go. Rob & Aliss have two grown up children and are proud grandparents.

@alisscresswell

CONTENTS

INTRODUCTION

It's been ten years since we opened our café in Chester UK. In my book, '**A Diary of Miracles Part One**' I tell the story of how we opened the café in our 'needy' neighborhood of Blacon and how miracles broke out the day we opened. '**A Diary of Miracles Part Two**' tells how we also opened a gift shop, 'Spirit', in Chester city center, and documents the miracles as they continued.

We've witnessed hundreds, if not thousands of miracles of lives being transformed over the past ten years, not just in Chester, but everywhere we go. For many of those who receive a miracle, whether it's an encounter on a plane, or in a shop, it's a brief meeting and so we don't get to see them again. However, many have kept in touch with us and we've had the privilege of seeing the remarkable transformations lived out.

I wanted to let some of those people share their inspirational stories with you to give you hope, and not only that, but also an opportunity to receive a miracle for yourself.

I interviewed each person and took video and audio recordings, and then (with the help of Phoenix and Oliver – thank you!) transcribed their stories. I spent time editing each story to make them easier for you to read. I changed some of the order and some words to make the stories flow grammatically and chronologically but I also left each person's vocabulary unchanged as much as possible including slang words, to keep them authentic.

At the beginning of each story I explain how I know the person and how we met. I also include a prayer for you to pray at the end of every chapter if you wish. Try to read the prayer out loud if you can and you'll be surprised by what begins to happen in your own life as you do.

Read the stories and if, like me, you relate to anything you read, whether it be an emotion, an experience or a need, then open up your heart and let any negative feelings go. You may find you become emotional when you least expect it, but don't be afraid or embarrassed, you will find something good happens when you open up. Read these powerful true stories, discover how they occurred and get ready to receive breakthrough in your own life.

Aliss Cresswell

March 2019

From the mountains of North Wales

Chapter One

SARAH

Introducing Sarah

I first met Sarah when I was twelve years old. We were both 'new girls' at a school in Chester. I'd moved from Frodsham High School, about ten miles away when my parents relocated and it was my first day at this large suburban High School. I remember the feelings of apprehension the night before and nervousness when I woke up on the morning of my first day. I was thankful to meet another girl who was new in the class that day as her parents had also moved to Chester. Her name was Sarah.

Sarah's story could fill a whole book on its own, or in fact many books, but I wanted to let her share some of it here in her own words. Even though I know her well, I was surprised to learn new facts as I interviewed her for this book. As you read her story, you'll be amazed at the ways in which God keeps her safe, preserves her life and how 'He makes all things work together for the good of those who love Him and follow Him' (see Romans 8:28).

As you read the following chapters, ask the Holy Spirit to show you how He has also been working in your life to bring you through times of trouble and adversity and trust Him for your breakthrough too, no matter what you need!

SARAH'S STORY

I grew up on a dairy farm in Cheshire, England in the nineteen seventies. My parents worked hard: my dad was a bit of a loner, and almost never left the farm, and my mum ran around, always taking on too much. As a result, when I came along, I was left to my own devices.

I remember the little girl who lived next door to us. She used to have toys and dolls. I didn't have any of that stuff, but for my third birthday, my dad went out of his way to get me a pony, and he sacrificed a lot to send me for riding lessons.

Before she met my dad, my mum used to be quite normal. She played the piano, helped at local schools, taught typing and shorthand, and enjoyed all sorts of things. But once she married my dad and was living and working on the farm bringing up three children, there was no time left for things she wanted to do. Also, my dad had some odd ideas. I remember one birthday, instead of a present she really wanted, he gave her a load of pigs!

Before they were married, my mother loved to play the piano, but my father had an aversion to any type of music, so he kept the piano locked and wouldn't let her play it. She managed to put the radio on sometimes, but only when he was out milking the cows and couldn't hear it. I wasn't allowed any type of music either, until I was a teenager, and got myself a cassette player.

I was restricted from socializing too. I couldn't bring the few friends I had to the farm because it was too dangerous for children and my parents never had time to take me anywhere, so I was pretty much cut off from normal life. Ours wasn't a normal family; we didn't go on holiday together, I didn't sit on my mum's knee or hear either of them tell me they loved me. I spent time with the horses and my parents spent time trying to keep on top of the farm. It was hardly the family I wanted.

When I was twelve, we moved to a bigger farm near Chester, about thirty miles from our previous farm. Things changed a lot when we moved there. I didn't have the same connections that I had in my hometown which was something I found difficult. That was when I met Aliss, the other new girl at the High School. She had a horse, so we used to go riding together, sometimes for a whole day. I remember when the M53 motorway was being built, there was sand for miles, and we would canter through it all day without a care in the world, feeling totally free; it was exhilarating. I loved those days out riding. Sometimes we took part in local horse shows and that was fun, doing show jumping and trying to beat the clock without knocking down a pole.

Aliss and I went out riding together often, but there was always one time each week when Aliss couldn't ride. This was when her family went to church. My mum only went to church twice a year and my dad probably managed it twice in his lifetime. Aliss invited me to her church a few times and I enjoyed going. It had something genuine and I liked the Bible stories and hearing about Jesus doing miracles, but I wondered, "Where are all the miracles today?" I wanted my life to change, and I remember asking, "God, if you're real, please do something."

By the time I was a teenager, my parents were finding it difficult to cope with me. I don't think I was particularly rebellious, but they just didn't know how to parent a teenager. They started to become more forceful and were often physically abusive. I was injured a few times due to the physical abuse and then began to retaliate rather than just take the beatings, which caused some injuries to them as well. I hated it at home and tried to run away but failed.

I went into Chester city center one day with Aliss when we were fourteen and we bought some temporary hair dye – just 'wash in, wash out' hair color that you do yourself at home. I put it in my hair and they were so angry that they took me to the police station and told the police they didn't want me anymore. I felt like my world was falling apart.

Soon after that, when I was almost fifteen, I met John who was seventeen. He was my first love. We met one day when I rode my pony down his street to see my school friend Tracy. I really liked John and we got on well. Tracy agreed to send notes back and forth from John to arrange times for us to meet. He was so sweet with me and we saw each other most days for a while. However, things were becoming very difficult for me at home and I didn't want to live there any longer. I wanted to be with John, but one day while I was at John's parents' house with him, the police arrived and took me back home to the farm and I was prevented from seeing John anymore. That broke my heart.

My parents said they'd had enough of me. They invited a vicar round, and then social workers. I didn't really understand what was going on but finally, for various reasons, I ended up going into foster care. Social services found me a home where I could take my horse. When I arrived at the home of my new foster parents, I was surprised to see a photograph on the mantelpiece of a couple who were involved in the church that Aliss had taken me to. It was completely unconnected but gave me a sense of hope. My carers were atheists, but the Christian couple in the photo were close family and this really helped me.

During that time, I was able to go to Bible camp and even got baptized fully in water, which caused uproar with my parents. Looking back, I can see how God gave me these opportunities. I lost touch with

Aliss when we were seventeen as she left home and went away to college. I tried to move back in with my parents, but it didn't work out. I was too old to go into foster care, so I lived in various places including a boarding house, which the government paid for.

I tried many things to improve my life, but eventually it all became too much for me and I didn't want to go on living. I'd lost the love of my life, no one wanted me and I had no hope. I was seventeen. I decided to kill myself, so I took an overdose of painkillers, but despite the quantity of tablets I took, I survived the suicide attempt. However, a few weeks later when I was due to sit school exams, my skin turned yellow from a strain of hepatitis caused by the overdose. I didn't tell anyone about the overdose so the doctor diagnosed me with glandular fever.

I left school, and in my search to find somewhere to live and someone who loved me, I ended up in a three-year relationship with a man. We planned to get married and buy a house, but I felt that I couldn't go through with it, so I left him and moved back in with my parents at the farm. It was then that I learned I was pregnant.

I plucked up the courage to tell my mum about the baby. She was angry and told me that unless I had an abortion, she would kick me out of the house. But I just couldn't do it. So I left home again, spent a few months in a homeless hostel, and then managed to get a council flat in a high-rise block of flats. At that time, Aliss was visiting her family in Chester and found out where I was and came to visit me. She lived in a different part of the country so again we lost touch and that was the last time we saw each other for over two decades.

I had my first child at the age of twenty. I went to church when I could and I met a man who was older than me. Within two years we were married and I had my second child, but soon after this I was quite poorly with post-natal depression. It completely changed me as a person; the way I thought and felt. I wasn't myself, and at one point, it got so bad, I couldn't even make myself a cup of tea or look after my boys. I went to church for help, but the people there just said it was the 'baby blues' and not to worry. I felt like they didn't believe me, or take me seriously, which made me even worse. In the end, I had to battle the illness on my own. There were months of ups and downs, and then one day I just 'fell out' with God. I told him that if He didn't heal me, I wouldn't speak to Him again. He didn't, and so I didn't. For a very long time.

My husband had issues as well. He was bipolar, and with the depression I was suffering, I couldn't have been easy to live with either. I couldn't sit still or be in the house, so I went out all the time and eventually my husband changed the locks, so I left him. By this point, in my mid-twenties, I was planning another suicide attempt. I really, really meant this one and saved up all my medication for months. I was going to take the whole lot and I knew that would be it. I was so desperate, I made sure that nobody would find me. I was in a place by myself and knew that I was all alone. Just before I took all the pills I said, "God, if there is a hell, don't let me die." Then I took the whole amount of medication and waited for death to come.

But something extraordinary happened and death did not come. That night, as I lay dying, a miracle took place, although I didn't realize it at the time. I'd made sure that I wouldn't be found, but believe it or not, a burglar decided to break into my home at the exact same time that I lay there dying! He stumbled across my unconscious body, called an ambulance, and the next thing I knew, I was waking up in hospital, attached to all kinds of machines and tubes. But I didn't see it as a miracle or as an answer to prayer - I was furious! I was so mad, I tried to rip the tubes out and smash up the monitors. All I wanted to do was to get out before a psychiatrist got to me, so I could try and kill myself again. I felt that I had nothing to live for. I had to leave hospital in a wheelchair because I was still so drugged up, I couldn't walk.

Not long after this, I managed to get a job in fundraising and I was quite good at it, so I started making a bit of money. That's how I met another man and got into a relationship with him. The trouble was, he turned out to be violent. He said that if I didn't marry him, he would set fire to my boys' house and burn them. I didn't think I had a choice, so I ended up marrying him. He was jealous and possessive and, if anyone looked at me, he would physically attack them. I remember one time when we were driving along, he slammed on the breaks, jumped out of the car and stabbed someone on the pavement. I think he was paid as a hit man; it was awful, but I felt trapped with no escape and no-one to turn to.

One day he left some candles burning, then fell asleep and set the house on fire. He blamed it all on me, even though I had nothing to do with it. Not long after this he went to prison and while he was in there, I escaped. I left with my dog and went into hiding. I stayed in other people's houses and even changed my name. I was scared, but I had to do it. I managed to get a new job, and through a staff party, I met a man who started to look after me. He was rebuilding some flats and said I could live there with my boys, so I did. My violent ex-husband came looking for me. He went to my work and threatened my boss with a pick-axe handle, and once he even came to the door of where I lived, but my new partner was able to protect me.

Things began to settle down for a while and me and my new partner had two children: a son and a daughter, and after ten years of being together we got married. Soon after that, we sold our home and moved to the USA and had another daughter.

Moving to the States was scary for me. It made me think more about our marriage. I realized that I had no safety net and, even after ten years, I wasn't sure how I felt about having no way out. I was thirty-six by now, with five kids, having just started my third marriage. This uneasiness and unhappiness grew. I bought self-help books and I tried lots of things, but everything just seemed to collapse around me, all the time, no matter what I tried.

One day, I got so exhausted and sick of it all that I turned to God. For the first time, I spoke to Him properly, and I told Him that I needed a miracle. I then discovered that our next-door neighbors there in Florida followed Jesus. They often took my nine-year-old son on fishing trips, and one day he asked if he could go with them to church. I agreed and realized I needed to start going to church again myself, to make some changes and get my life in order, but I was afraid to leave the house for too long. My husband was very particular. If one thing, even a box of cereal, was out of place and I wasn't around to find it for him, then there would be trouble. The idea of spending a whole morning at church scared me; it could be more hassle than it was worth.

While I was wrestling with all this, an amazing thing happened. Aliss was still living in England and I was in America and we hadn't seen each other for twenty something years. But out of the blue, the Holy Spirit asked Aliss to pray for me. So she prayed and said, "Wherever Sarah is in the whole world, I pray that she would really know you Jesus. Holy Spirit, I ask that you get her and not let her go!" She had no idea where I was or what I was doing.

Two days later, without knowing any of this, I suddenly felt that I wanted to talk to Aliss. I managed to track her down and spoke to her over the phone for the first time in over two decades. I heard about the crazy things she and her husband, Rob, were doing: going wherever the Holy Spirit sent them and seeing visions, miracles, and lives changed. I wanted that. I wanted that kind of relationship with God. To be with Him in real life; not just sitting on a pew but having an adventure!

I wanted to see people talking about Jesus in cafés, just like Aliss was doing back in England. So I asked God to do that for me, then I got in my car with my youngest son and I drove. I didn't know where I was going but after about thirteen miles the Holy Spirit told me to pull over and I stopped at a restaurant. Just after we were seated, a man at the table next to ours started talking about Jesus, right in front of me. I could hardly believe it. It turned out he belonged to the church that my son attended too! It really was quite amazing.

This gave me the push I needed to go to church. I went forward in the meeting that Sunday and gave my life to Jesus properly; this time I meant it. I couldn't wait to go back the following week. But Saturday night, one of my kids threw up so I couldn't go. The next week, the same thing happened, again the night before church. I didn't think this was a coincidence, so I prayed. I did manage to go to church for about a month after that, even the midweek meetings. It was wonderful. I was praying for things and they were just falling into my hands.

Unfortunately, around this time, a big argument erupted at my house between my husband, myself, and my eldest son. The nearest store was ten miles away, and we had run out of bread. My husband started cursing me and telling me it was my fault he couldn't have his cooked breakfast. My son began shouting back, and before long, my husband told him to get out of his house and never come back. I remember them both looking at me, each expecting me to back them up. I didn't know what to say, and it all just felt wrong, so I prayed.

As a result, I didn't react the way I normally would have done. I think this infuriated my husband even more. He said that I had twenty-four hours to make my son leave and that if he came back the next day and found him still there, he would sell the house and leave the country, abandoning me there with five children. I would have no money, no home and no hope of work or state benefits, as I was on his visa. He then went outside, smashed the windshield of my car and left.

The next day, I drove to church with a smashed windshield. I hid the car so nobody would see it. In the meeting, the Pastor got a word of knowledge, something he couldn't have known naturally. He stood up and said, "There's a woman here with a situation at home. It's completely out of your control and isn't your fault. I'd like that person to come to the front." It was a huge deal for me, but there were other people going forward, so I went up and tried to hide in the crowd. But then, when the Pastor reached me, something happened I couldn't understand. I remember there was some serious praying, spiritual stuff started happening around me and demonic things were being dealt with. I remember feeling something like a big raindrop land on my face and thinking someone was trying to put holy water on me until I realized it was spiritual, not physical. There was nothing there you could see, but supernaturally, water was landing on me.

I discovered that God wanted to give me an anointing of the Holy Spirit to deal with the situation at home. He came down, met with me, and gave me what I needed. I went back to my husband and he asked what I had decided to do about my son. I replied that I wasn't going to do anything, so my husband told me he was going to leave me and demanded his passport. I wouldn't get it for him, so he called the police. He went out to the garden to wait for them, and left me in the house, terrified.

I prayed desperately, and as I looked down, I

could see something in my hands. It was a vision, but it looked real: I was holding a royal flush, the highest hand in poker. I realized that my husband was calling me 'all in' with our house, our marriage and everything, just like in poker. This was the first time I really had to stand by faith for what I believed was God's will. It was the biggest gamble of my life so far.

Within minutes, four big officers came to the door with their guns. I remember praying that at least one of them would know Jesus and would be able to see into the situation. One of them came in and told me to give over the passport. I held up my hands and did my best to tell my side of the story. He listened to me. When I'd finished, he turned to the other officers and said something to them. He asked me what I wanted to happen. I explained that I just wanted to sit down with a counsellor and sort all this out.

The officer nodded and took control of the situation, asking questions and taking statements. In the middle of my statement, I blurted out that my husband thought he was God. I will never forget what happened next. The officer stood up, opened his mouth, and before I knew it, he was prophesying over the house! He said that there was only one God and that every knee would bow to Him, and Him alone. He said that I was not to bow down, or back down, to the man in this house. It freaked me out no end. I asked the officer who he was, but he didn't answer.

Then I looked out of the window, and for the first time, I saw what was happening in the spirit realm. It was an open vision, like a movie in full color. I saw my husband with strings, like he was some sort of puppet, and he was leading people into hell. I shouted out for it to stop and one of the strings broke. He lost control and spun around, losing his footing, and the people started to escape. I was terrified at this point, as you can imagine.

The officer turned to me and said he was going to leave but would send someone back to help. I later found out that this officer used to Pastor a local church. He had once been married to a witch, until he found Jesus. Apparently, one evening, after hosting a Bible study, his wife's cat sat on his lap and spoke to him in an audible voice! It asked why he was bringing Christians into the house. Needless to say, this man threw the cat to the floor and moved away. He gave his life to Jesus and later became a Pastor, and then a police officer with a particular reputation for dealing with paranormal incidents.

The lady he sent to help us was a child protection officer. She talked to all the members of the family and said that there was still hope. She recommended counselling, which is what I'd wanted in the first place. It turned out this lady followed Jesus too, and her church offered free counselling sessions. We went along and met with the Pastor a few times. We had to bind up a lot of evil spirits and then my husband was hit hard by the Holy Spirit. He said he wanted Jesus in his life and he decided to come with me to church the next day. However, that night, our kids threw up again, and something broke in our plumbing. We had sewage coming up through the toilet and it flooded the floors. I remember standing there in the early hours of the morning, feeling just like I was in the middle of a horror movie – sewage bubbling up under my feet and children vomiting around me! The enemy did not want us in that church. But we did go.

It was a constant struggle, always praying for everything. I couldn't remember anyone else having to pray so much just to get to church. It helped that my husband invited Jesus into his life, but we still had a lot of dramas. One episode was when my husband took on a new employee in his business that we'd met at church. She was actually a witch, disguising herself as a Christian. She came into our house a lot and I knew she wanted to ruin our family. I saw all this in the spirit but could never prove anything. My husband started to take her side and it got to a point when I almost left, but God told me I had to stay. During this time, I felt like I was playing chess. I couldn't win the game myself, but God was showing me what to do, move by move. Then, one day, I was given a prophetic word from someone about a chess board: that the necessary pieces had been taken from the board and things were lined up at last. By the next day, the witch had gone. That was one battle the Lord asked me to stay in, but there were others which He told me to leave.

(Sarah's story continues in chapter two).

Chapter Two
SARAH'S STORY
Continued

Whilst all this was happening, I was in regular contact with Aliss. She helped and encouraged me over the phone to keep following Jesus. One day, out of the blue she answered her front door in Chester England, and there I was, standing there with my suitcases and my two youngest kids, with no husband and no home. The local council advised me not to stay with friends and said I would be awarded a council house more quickly if I was 'homeless' so they sent me to a women's refuge about twenty miles away in North Wales.

The Lord had made it clear that I needed to go back to England, so I was trying to be obedient. He showed me a building in a dream, and when I was taken to the refuge, I recognized it as being the same place. Even though it was not ideal, at least I had peace that it was where I needed to be. In this place were a lot of troubled women. I think they saw the peace that I had and were confused by it. They asked many questions and opened up when I talked to them. The only answer I ever really had for them was Jesus.

One night a woman at the refuge injured her foot. I didn't want to drive to Accident & Emergency as it was late, so I began to tell her that Jesus could heal it and how Aliss could pray for her the following day. However, she didn't want to wait until the next day and was in so much pain, she was demanding that I did the miracle! I had talked about miracles so much as I'd seen Aliss do them, but now here I was, on the spot, in front of everybody. I felt stupid and scared, but I prayed, and to my amazement, her pain vanished and the swelling and bruising disappeared instantly!

This kicked off all sorts of drama. I saw more miracles and started leading some of the women to faith in Jesus. It caused trouble with other people, and the staff threatened to kick me out if I kept talking about Jesus. I brought many of the women to the church and café where Aliss was. There was one girl who had been a heroin addict, until she gave her life to Jesus one Sunday morning. She asked for a Bible, and Aliss gave her one, but as soon as she placed it in her hand, the girl threw it back at her! Aliss tried again and again, but whenever this girl touched the word of God, the Bible would vibrate so much with the power of God, she would jump and drop it.

For the next ten months, while waiting for a home of my own, I lived at the refuge with my two girls and this sort of thing happened all the time. I took women to the café and saw them give their lives to Jesus and delivered from things I didn't even know existed. All the while, I had no home, no money, and no stability. My husband, still in America, had decided he was gay and divorced me. To this day, I am amazed at how God managed to make so much good come out of so much chaos. But things weren't easy by any means.

By this time, my eldest son was twenty-one-years-old and had also moved back to England. For about a week I had a strange feeling that he was in trouble. Sure enough, one night, he called me at four thirty in the morning. I asked what was going on, but he said he couldn't tell me. He was so distraught, I thought he might have had a car accident or hurt someone. I kept asking, but we went around in circles, and so eventually I suggested he take half an hour to calm down and said that I would call him right back.

He told me that he loved me, and I said I loved him too, then he ended the call. During this half hour, I was in and out of sleep, but I had two visions of him; the kind you hope are just your imagination. I phoned back half an hour later like I'd said, but he didn't pick up. I kept trying but I could not get in touch with him. This went on all day, until six-o-clock in the evening. It was then that I started getting strange phone calls, asking if I had heard from my family. My parents had both died some time before this, and I had lost contact with other family members, so I started to realize something bad had happened. I thought back to the two visions I had seen in the night.

They found my son's body at three-o-clock that afternoon. I was one of the last to know because the refuge where I lived was in a secret location. The police eventually got through to me and explained that he had committed suicide. One of the first people I spoke to was Aliss. She asked me where his body was and if I had thought about trying to resurrect him from the dead, just like people did in the Bible. She was keen to go to the hospital and I said I would accompany her, along with our friend Linda. So off we went to the mortuary, and with a Police Officer looking on, we prayed over my son for half an hour. It must have looked very strange, but we wanted to give him ample opportunity to come back from the dead. Sadly, he didn't. I felt as though my heart would break. But I remembered that my son had asked Jesus into his life when he was a young boy, and perhaps now that he was with Him face to face, he would not be so keen to come back to us.

I was well looked after in the days that followed. I felt the enemy trying to control the situation, but God spoke to me in many ways and through many people. Aliss' husband Rob conducted the funeral – it was the first one he'd done, and I asked him to tell the people there about Jesus and give them opportunity to know Him. Some of my son's friends confirmed that my son had never stopped believing in God. If he did know Jesus, then that probably explains why he didn't want to come back, and that thought was a comfort to me.

I finally got the keys to a council house, just two

weeks after the funeral, in the run up to Christmas. I remember standing in the kitchen and, despite being relieved that I finally had my own home, I felt like something was attacking me. It wouldn't stop, and I heard God tell me that I needed to fast from food, so I did. Two days before the end of the fast, I was at a School of the Spirit meeting, and it became clear to me I needed to repent and trust God again. I got home and did just that.

Immediately, I felt the demon go. It was like this great black thing rushed out of me, and I was filled with joy. I started singing and laughing. Then, on the last day of the fast, I was in my kitchen again. For only the third time in my life I heard Jesus speak to me in an audible voice. He called my name and asked if I would take communion with Him before I broke my fast. Well, I could hardly say no, could I!? I asked Him when, and He said whenever I was ready, so I got together some bread and some wine, and He talked me through it. I couldn't see Him, but He spoke to me. He said how the bread was His body, broken for me. He stressed that point and used my name when He spoke. He then said the wine was His blood, and as He told me to drink it, it looked thicker and more like blood than before. He said there is power in His blood and that power is in me.

That week, He showed me many things. A lot of people probably thought I was crazy, and worried I'd finally lost it, but I was secure. Within a few weeks, I knew He wanted me to spend time at the café with Aliss. I started working there three days a week. I thought I was just going to make cups of tea, but Aliss encouraged me and I ended up leading people to Jesus and seeing many miracles. I think working there was just as much help to me as to the people I served.

It was around this time that I met Mandi, whose amazing story is also told in this book. She was in and out of prison, stacking up nearly two-hundred offences, until she came into the café and met with Jesus in a dramatic way. Her journey since has been up and down: professionals couldn't handle her, and no rehabilitation center could take her, and eventually, I heard God ask me to take her in myself. That step of faith wasn't plain sailing, but I found a lot of purpose looking after her.

And now I've entered another chapter of my life. It's funny how, when you follow Jesus, He works everything out, even though at the time you can't see the wood for the trees. Remember the young man, John who was my first love, but we were forced to separate as teenagers? Well, listen to this and see how God has been faithful in my life as I've been following Him:

A few years ago, after I gave my life to Jesus and when I was single again, I had a clear vision of God bringing me a wonderful husband. I only saw the back of his head and God had His own hands wrapped around me like He was hiding me from this guy. And then suddenly God opened His hands from around me and kind of snagged this guy quickly into my life. So I knew when I did meet him, it was to happen super-fast. Sometime later, a couple of friends prayed for my future husband to come into my life. One of them felt that something had been stolen from me when I was young and God was going to bring it back. They had no idea about my first love, John.

The following month, just before Christmas, I had visions of a winter fairytale and of an engagement ring. I knew God was telling me He was going to keep His promise to me. I asked God for my future husband to come and find me, but I had no idea who it would be. I knew that we were being hidden from each other as that's what I'd seen in the vision. Then out of the blue, two days before Christmas, I received a Facebook friend request from John and recognized him straight away. We ended up chatting over the phone on Christmas Eve and it turned out that his daughter had found out about his teenage romance with me. She had decided to try and reunite us after all these years, at the exact same time I'd prayed for my future husband to be revealed!

Unbeknown to me, John had been praying that if we were meant to marry, then God would show me, and of course He did. It soon became clear that John and I had been in close proximity to each other for years but not actually had the opportunity to meet. He used to sit in his friend's garden which backed onto mine – neither of us had a clue that we were just feet apart, separated only by a fence! And as a taxi driver, he would often help his elderly customers in and out of Aliss' café where I worked, but we still hadn't noticed each other. Then I too became a taxi driver for a while, but our paths didn't cross. One day, John did manage to find out where I lived, but while he was plucking up the courage to knock on the door, I moved to a new house in the next town!

Anyway, we met up just before midnight on Christmas Eve 2016 for a few moments. It was so romantic. There was still a spark between us after all those years and the Lord then showed me in a dream that I was to marry him. We met up again and John was saying the same things to me word for word that Jesus had said to me. This was blowing me away, especially when I realized that he was the person I had seen in the visions a few years back.

I introduced John to my children and they all liked him straight away. Then John started to have dreams of us getting married on a sunny day with all my family, (including my ex-husband) and my church friends together at the wedding. We got engaged and planned to get married at Little Mollington Hall at Easter. That was the house that Aliss and Rob were running as a boutique B&B and where I was then working as housekeeper.

We had a wonderful wedding. Amazingly it was a sunny day and we were able to get married in the beautiful gardens. My ex-husband's family did the catering, wedding cake, cars, hair and make-up. A friend found me a dress which was bought within ten minutes of discussion over a coffee. Everything came together so well. Rob and Aliss did the blessing and some of my friends organized the photos and the decorations. We could hardly believe all the love everyone showed to us.

And now, as the fairytale continues, John and I find ourselves running Little Mollington Hall and hosting other people's weddings. Rob and Aliss set up the business and then passed it over to us. It really is like a dream come true. God is so faithful.

If you find yourself in a similar place to where I was, perhaps you've turned your back on God, or you're in a situation that is desperate and out of your control, I would say this: God is real. If you ask Him to show you, He will prove it to you. You really must go after Him, but He will show Himself to you. Just don't waste any more time! Ask Him to come into your life and get around people who walk with Him. It might take a few days or weeks to get that connection, but once you get it, it will blow your mind. So, wherever you are, whatever you're doing, I pray that you would find that real, good, God-connection. May He touch you, and bless you, and fill your life!

Pray with Aliss:

"Father God, help me to make wise choices, that I may know your good plans for my life and not go my own way. Please speak to me through visions and dreams like you did with Sarah and show me the reality of the spiritual realm around me. Thank you that even though the enemy has tried to steal good things from my life, that through You, those things can be restored. I pray for full restoration of anything that the enemy has stolen from me or my family as I submit my life to Jesus Christ. Help me to trust you no matter what the circumstances look like. In the name of Jesus, Amen."

Chapter Three
MARK
Introducing Mark

The first time I remember meeting Mark was at one of our workshops in Fort Mill, South Carolina. He'd driven from Wilmington, North Carolina, around four hours away. I explained that Wilmington was where I'd done my first miracle in 2006; a woman's deaf ear was instantly healed as I called out a word of knowledge in a meeting there.

During the Fort Mill workshop, I was impressed with Mark's prophetic insight when he was praying with other people. I assumed he'd been following Jesus for decades as he seemed to really know God and had a strong prophetic gifting, coupled with wisdom and insight into God's ways.

I was surprised to learn later that he only began following Jesus relatively recently. He invited Rob, me and our team to host a Supernatural Workshop and 'Expect a Miracle' night in his hometown of Wilmington. It was there that I got to know Mark and his wife Charlotte. As soon as I heard his incredible story, I asked him to tell me more about his background. Mark and I sat outside his family's restaurant, 'Dockside', with spectacular views over the waterway as he told me his story. As you read this, open up your heart to receive Father God's love through His Holy Spirit, no matter how unworthy you may feel.

MARK'S STORY

I grew up in Wilmington, North Carolina - between Wilmington and Topsail. My parents were only nineteen when they had me; they'd eloped to get married when they were young. My grandfather was the Grand Master Freemason. He was the highest-ranking Mason in the area. As I grew up, he treated me like a king. I was told that my birth changed the pattern of his life. He called me 'Big Man' and I called him 'Big Pa'. I was outgoing and smart but very spoiled.

My grandfather and father had a law firm here in Wilmington. My parents sent me to a private school because they believed education to be the highest form of advancement. But private school was traumatic for me. I was humiliated and teased for everything I was seen to be deficient in. I kept all my feelings bottled up which profoundly affected me, and the happy, well-adjusted child that I had been, was lost.

I was destined to carry on the family name and become a lawyer, but it just wasn't for me because I preferred being outdoors, so I went into real estate development with my father. We ended up being quite successful here in this area. We invested in more and more property and our business went from strength to strength. We made a lot of money. We had everything we could ever want. We had a lot of real estate. We owned a lot of property in North Carolina and other states. I had everything I could possibly want: airplanes, boats, a home in Aspen and yet there was just this void in me.

Money became a big issue, along with acceptance and pleasing others. I pretended to be someone I was not, with everyone, including my family. I didn't know who I was and lost my true identity. I carried shame and guilt for not being able to become a lawyer and please my family. I ruined my first marriage by putting myself and everything I wanted first. And I lost the relationship I should have had with my first daughter.

Money fixed all, or so I thought, and I sunk deeper into its clutches. Big Pa had told me one day I would be wealthy and I would inherit all that the family owned. We did become wealthy, but our family remained dysfunctional. We prospered and lived the 'American dream'. We thought we didn't need God for anything – we could buy our way out of any problems we faced.

I remarried, and for a while, things were looking up. We were thrilled to find out my wife was pregnant with our first daughter together. But tragedy struck, and our daughter was stillborn. I was devastated but I wouldn't let anyone know how I was feeling. Thankfully, my wife threw herself on God and gave her life to Jesus. But I did not.

I sank into depravity and pulled further away. I was lying and consumed with the spirit of lust. I started to drink and take drugs and continued seeking after money, power and prestige, following my own desires.

My wife and I had a second daughter together and our wealth increased. Outwardly all looked well, but inwardly I was dying. Shame, guilt, pride and the love of money were eating away at my health and happiness. I couldn't understand why I was acting the way I did. I felt helpless and could not stop. I hated myself because of it.

Then came the financial crash. During the 2008 real estate depression, we were one of the many businesses caught up in the debacle and we lost everything. All our wealth and everything that went with it; all that we had built up. I know what it is to have everything money can buy and what it is to hit rock bottom. I didn't cope with it well at all. My wealth was everything to me – my foundation and my identity. Up until this point, my life was centered around money. It involved plenty of travelling and living the typical jet-set lifestyle.

My father had to file for bankruptcy. You hear stories of people going from rags to riches, but this was the complete opposite. When money is your lord, and your identity and purpose and your everything, when it goes, you don't know who you are. I didn't know who I was and felt stripped of everything. Fear, anxiety and desperation set in because I had no rock to stand on at that time.

I found myself on a path of self-destruction. I began drinking excessively and started using hard drugs. My wife, Charlotte stuck with me through all the mess of my life. I would lock myself in my office, drowning my unhappiness with alcohol, taking drugs and watching pornography. At the same time, she would lie prostrate on the floor outside my office door, praying that God would save me. I owe so much to her. I would often think, "Why am I doing these things?" I had great parents and a wonderful wife and family and yet I was on a path of destruction and didn't seem able to stop. Several times I thought I was going to have a heart attack. But I kept on using. My life was spiralling out of control and things got so bad that I was on course to be dead within three months. Something had to change, and it needed to happen quickly.

But it wasn't what I expected. In May 2010 my sister contacted me and told me that she had non-Hodgkin's lymphoma: cancer. I was devastated. My first thought was that it was my fault and God was punishing my family because of me. I wanted to help her but didn't know what to do.

There were two things she asked me to help with. One was to see if I would be a match for a bone marrow transplant. I agreed, and the bone marrow test kit arrived in the mail. As soon as I picked up the kit, I heard God speak to me for the first time. The Holy Spirit said to me, "You're a perfect match." I didn't even know God at that time, but He spoke so clearly into my mind. So I did the swab and sent it in and after ten days I called them up. They told me that my sister hadn't even sent hers in at that point, so I called her up and told her to hurry up because I knew I was a match. A couple of weeks later I received a phone call. They explained that twins are normally a 96% match, but that me and my sister, not even twins, were a 99% match. I knew this was God.

The other thing she asked me to do would impact my life dramatically. She told me about a Christian Healing conference in Jacksonville, Florida and asked me to go with her. Of course, I agreed, even though I had no relationship with God and was living a totally opposing lifestyle.

My sister's plea for help came at just the right time and was to instigate a huge transformation in my life that was unprecedented. Those three months prior to the trip were intense. My drug taking escalated, I became more withdrawn and things got really ugly. The night before we left, I stayed up all night using drugs and barely made the plane.

I sensed something was going to happen in Florida although I didn't know what. The Lord was calling me to Him. I had always believed in God and when I was young, attended an Episcopal Church, but I never knew you could have a personal relationship with the Lord and to be honest, I hadn't given it much thought.

In August 2010 we flew down to Jacksonville to attend the Christian Healing conference. As soon as we arrived, I headed straight to the hotel bar and ordered myself some martinis. I then searched out a strip club where I stayed until closing time. Emerging from there at 3.00 am, I needed to get back to the hotel, but I was stuck. I tried calling a cab, but my phone died, and I was out in the middle of nowhere, alone. I was stranded in the worst part of town and was about to be mugged. I was wearing a $30,000 watch and had about $10,000 cash in my pocket. I sat on a curb as a car drove past slowly. Fear overtook me and in desperation I cried out, "God, get me back to my hotel and I'll take this seriously."

I was stunned as an off-duty cab pulled up, just at that moment. The driver rolled down his window and shouted, "Man, are you crazy? You could get killed out here." I was so grateful as he took me back to my hotel. I went to bed for a few hours' sleep and then made it to the conference a little late. As I walked into the meeting, powerful worship music was playing. The only worship I'd heard before was hymns; I'd never experienced anything like this. The reason I'd gone to this Christian conference was because my sister with cancer had asked me to go with her. The Lord had tricked me! He used my sister to get me there but I knew nothing of His wonderful plans for me at that point.

As soon as I experienced the worship I began to cry. The power of God hit me, although I didn't realize it was the power at that time, but I could feel it. He began to cleanse me. I cried through everything that day: as I was eating my hamburger for lunch I cried and eating my dinner that evening I cried. Something was happening to me!

My sister had arranged a prayer ministry session for herself at the conference and took me with her. Of course, since I had grown up with her, I knew her well, but the people that were ministering to her were complete strangers. However, during the session they began to tell her things they couldn't possibly have known naturally, and yet I knew them to be true. It was just blowing my mind.

They were getting words of knowledge about her life and were speaking in tongues which I'd never heard before and were praying for her. I didn't quite know what it was, but I could feel a sense that something dramatic was going to happen to me. And I sensed that I had to do something before it would happen. So I asked if I could have a session just like my sister and they booked me in for the following day at 5.30pm.

We were in a big conference and there were people all over the place, but the following afternoon me and my sister sat down with the two prayer ministers for my session; a man and a woman. I was convinced that I had sinned too much to be forgiven and worried they were not going to be able to help me. They gave me a booklet to fill out where I had to write down all the things that I'd been involved with. All my wrong doings! I began to write down my sins – there was a lot of sin to write about but I wanted to be honest. I looked down at what I'd written and I thought this God must be really something if He can turn this around. I burst into tears when I saw how bad I was on paper. I even threw it down onto the table and let my sister read it. I wanted to be very transparent. At that point I wanted to change and I can't begin to tell you the dramatic change that happened in my life that day. It was phenomenal.

I handed the booklet to the lady after I'd finished writing in it. She read through all the dreadful things that I was involved with. Suddenly she stood up, and with tears in her eyes, left the table where we were sitting and faced the corner of the room. I thought, 'I knew it. I'm cooked and I'm going to hell!'

The man put his hands on my shoulders and began to pray in tongues. As he did so, I could feel things moving around in me. Then the woman came back and asked if anyone in my family was a Freemason. I told her my grandfather was a thirty-third degree Mason. She replied, "The Holy Spirit has shown me that you were dedicated to the Masonic spirit, the spirit of Freemasonry when you were young and this is the cause of all the turmoil in your life. It's why you've tried to be good but are unable to and have ended up doing all these lascivious things."

I was shocked. How did she know that? Our family had been proud of their Masonic history. My grandfather was at the top level and would conduct secret Masonic meetings at our farmhouse. I hadn't known about being dedicated to the Masonic spirit at the time, but it made sense. I had been living under a curse. She asked me if I wanted to be free from that control to which I replied, "Yes."

With the help of the ministry team, I began to speak out renunciations where I renounced what I had been involved in and all the things I had been doing that were contrary to God's plan for my life. It was weird because I could hear myself saying words that I didn't understand and I could hear a dialect, almost like a different language, coming out of my mouth as I began to receive ministry. It sounded like Arabic or something although I knew it was English, but it sounded like someone else speaking.

At this point I began to weep again and started to sweat profusely. I felt weak and thought I would fall from the chair. The woman told me to stop as soon as I felt I was OK. I read almost to the end of the six-page booklet and said, "I think I'm good." Immediately she scooted her chair around and put her face so close to me that the end of her nose was almost touching mine. She sternly called my name, "Mark, Mark!" and then the third time she shouted, "Mark!" I literally felt something pop. I said, "What?" and she replied, "Finish the back page." On that final page was the last renunciation I had to speak out and it was to renounce the thirty-third degree, the top level of the Freemasonry in my family line. I renounced it but I don't remember what happened next.

I woke up forty-five minutes later. My sister was still there thankfully, and she was able to relate to me what had happened during that time. When I came to, I found I was covered in my own bodily fluids - snot, tears, sweat and stuff! Apparently, I'd been manifesting demons and they were leaving me throughout that time, but I remembered nothing about it. There were caring people around me, praying for me. It was miraculous. After I came to, my sister hardly recognized me as the same person. I had been transformed and set free by Jesus. I remember standing up and as I did so, I had to hold onto the people around me because I felt so light; I thought I would literally float to the ceiling if I didn't hold on.

Someone asked if I wanted to accept Jesus into my life which I did right away, and as I walked out, people that knew me were saying, "Wow you look totally different; you're glowing!" I can't begin to tell you the transformation that took place. It was like my life, my mind, everything was renewed.

I had flown down to Jacksonville as one person and flew back as a totally different person. I got home and called a family meeting and put some things straight within my family. My wife, Charlotte was like, "Who are you?" I was so different from the man who had gone to Jacksonville just a few days earlier. It was a dramatic transition because immediately I despised worldly things.

The following morning after I arrived home, the Lord woke me up at 5.30am and I began to read the Bible. I read it cover to cover in thirty days. I wrote reams of notes and then I read the whole Bible again in about fifty days. It was supernatural because I could read so fast, yet I could also memorize the Scriptures that I was reading. I was absorbing everything. I could not wait to get up each morning. The Lord would tell me to get up at a certain time but I would get up even earlier as I couldn't wait. He began talking to me in such a way that the Scriptures would come alive for me and I could feel the transformation happening to me each day. After the first six or eight months of being saved I probably read the Bible all the way through, five or six times. I joined a local church, became an usher and started a discipleship class. And I had subsequent prayer and deliverance sessions that further enhanced my freedom.

My sister belonged to a Holy Spirit-filled church and was a Christian counsellor. Her Pastor had a dream that he was supposed to take me to a ministry on the West Coast of America called Bethel, to a Healing conference there. He called and invited me. My sister and her husband paid for my plane ticket. So we all flew out there and my friend Jim came too. I had an incredible experience there. At one point the leaders of the meeting were calling people to go up onto the stage and they were laying hands on people who then fell down under the power of the Holy Spirit. I was on the stage but the last one in line. I looked across and I could see my sister on the floor, along with the Pastor. Everyone else seemed to be on the floor except me.

Then one of the leaders, Bill Johnson, came over and looking at me said, "Before the end of the day, you're going to get so radically taken by the Holy Spirit, it's going to be a manifestation for all to see." I then walked about ten paces down the steps, off the stage and back down to the main floor of the convention center where there were around three thousand people. All of a sudden, my legs started to go. They began shaking and then I burst out laughing. It was a holy laughter and so loud that everyone turned and watched me and then I hit the ground. It was uncontrollable. I laughed so much that my shirt rode up under my chin and I lost my shoes!

I must have rolled around laughing so much that I ended up about fifty feet away, under chairs where some old ladies were sitting. They leaned over, pulled their long skirts up and peered down between their knees at me lying under there. They pointed at me and said, "You've got the Holy Spirit!" My good friend Jim had to come and slide me out from under the chairs. Then Bill Johnson and Randy Clark came over and asked where my Pastor was. I looked up and called him over. They advised him, "When you get him back home, put him into prayer ministry and deliverance." And that's how I started out in ministry for the Lord. I got saved at 5.30pm on August 6th, 2010 in Jacksonville, Florida. I went to Bethel in January 2012 and got filled with the Holy Spirit and then my journey really accelerated.

I was so fortunate to move so fast with the Lord. The power of God is incredible. The power of reformation, the power of redemption, the power of reconciliation – it's the power of Jesus. The power of His love, it can do miraculous things. My hope has been restored. I have found my true identity in Jesus and my purpose. My family relationships have been restored; trust and love have returned, and my heart is new.

I am so thankful for my sister who invited me to that first conference in Jacksonville. She later told me that the reason she invited me was not for her sake, but for my sake. She was expecting God to do something in my life and He did. Words cannot express how grateful I also am to my wife. She stuck with me through everything when most other women would have left. I was at another conference one time and someone who I didn't know told me, "You're alive because your wife lay on the floor outside the door of your office and prayed for you." And that's literally what she would do. She saved my life. God heard her prayers and He saved me. Do not underestimate the power of prayer.

Monetarily speaking, I've never had less than I have today. But I can tell you that I've never been happier or more fulfilled in my life than I am now. Over the past few years I have dedicated my life to serving God, spending time with Him and helping other people.

After I discovered the dangers of Freemasonry and how demonic it is, I've helped other people to get free, just like I did. I had been dedicated to the 'Masonic spirit' as a young boy and as a result the enemy had a hold on me. The only thing that could set me free was the blood and name of Jesus.

Freemasonry is extremely demonic and has a major sexual component; there's an Asherah pole, Baal worship and everything. A lot of the demonic practices you read about in the Old Testament are manifest in the Masonic spirit. It's alive and well today – I can testify to that from my own life. I've also encountered a lot of it in other people's lives since and helped them to get free from that spirit which has manifest through the generations.

After I got saved, the Lord told me He was going to give me His insight. He has given me the ability to look into a person's situation and see beyond it. I don't need to address the problem, I can see the end point and I speak into that which helps unlock people's situations and brings breakthrough. The Lord gives me words of knowledge that shock people who are tied up in unbelief. I get insight into which stronghold is binding a person, and how to break it. I had been in such bondage myself, and now getting to see others set free is so special to me. Initially, every time I went to do ministry with someone, I would cry through the whole thing because I would be sitting there saying, 'Holy Spirit please speak', and the love of the Lord would come into the room so strong that I would just weep the whole time. I still get emotional now – I love seeing others set free.

The Lord also uses me to help business people. They may have a business problem and need strategy or need to know how to move forward or want to become more profitable. I help them transition into God's Kingdom way of business. To bring heaven to earth and bring even Christian businesses into Kingdom businesses. To put the value back on the people and so the focus is not on the bottom line. It began with the Lord sending people to me who needed help. I would consult with them and it always seemed to be about the relationships within the company, about calling out the person that owned the company as the shepherd of the people, the employees.

For example, there was a guy with a healthcare business in Texas. I prayed for him and helped him get free and he asked me to speak into his business. It was the first time I'd done anything like that. The Lord downloaded strategy and wisdom to me especially for him. The crux of it was this: "Every fifth new customer that you get, do the work totally free." I shared that with him, amazingly he put it into practice and suddenly his business multiplied. He went from grossing $400,000 to millions of dollars a year. As a result, he sent me a check as a thank you and to sow into the ministry that the Lord was giving me.

Another time I spoke to a guy with a copper business. We advised him about 'going vertical', which means owning every part of your supply line so you're not reliant on anybody else, which helped him enormously. And now there's a real estate business I'm speaking into, but mainly what it all boils down to is relationship. The Lord showed me that commerce - His business, being about your Father's business, is all about people.

I would like to pray for you as you read this. I ask for the love of the Father to come, that you would know the Father's heart; the emotions that caused Jesus to leave His throne in heaven and look at His Dad and say, "I'll go." Just like the prophet Isaiah said, "Send me." I pray that you will know the Father's love, that it will fill you from the bottom of your feet to the top of your head, that it will give you a sense of courage and boldness, but most of all that love and peace that passes understanding will be yours.

Lord we ask for an infilling today of the Father's perfect love because His perfect love is Jesus. I pray that Jesus invades your life and I release impartation of the Father's love. If you do not know Jesus, please bring Jesus into your life, glorify God and watch Him raise you up. The Lord says, "I will lift up the humble" and He will, because He is *for* you. Every bit of discipline from Him, as the Apostle Paul said, it is all gain. So, I bless you with the love of the Father, in Jesus' name, Amen.

Pray with Aliss:

"Father God, thank you that the blood of Jesus Christ breaks the power of curses, and I ask you to set me free from any curse in my life, through sin or any other source. Please make it clear to me if there is any sin in my life; any part of my life that is not pleasing to you. I am sorry for doing or saying or thinking those things. I ask you to forgive me for.......... and wash me clean through the powerful blood of Jesus. Amen."

Unexpected Miracles

Chapter Four
ADRIAN

Introducing Adrian

My Dad, David, is always happy to share his faith with others, and in this case, it was Adrian. Very often when we share our faith, we don't know how our conversation has impacted that person. However, Adrian was so interested to hear about the miracles we'd been witnessing in our café that he came to find out more for himself.

When I first met Adrian, I didn't know he was a Psychic Medium, but I knew that his life was about to change radically. Read his story and discover just how radical that change was!

ADRIAN'S STORY

As far back as I can remember, I'd been fascinated with anything to do with ghosts and the paranormal. One day as a boy, me and my two sisters were messing about with a Ouija board and we asked, "Is anyone there?" We got our answer when the glass moved over to "Yes." All three of us pulled away from the glass and laughed, thinking it was a bit of fun, until the glass shot off the board and smashed. That was the start of a six-month period of poltergeist activity in our home: drawers were pulled open in the living room and we heard the sound of footsteps on the stairs in the dead of night, but no-one was there. It came to a head when my eldest sister woke up one night with someone's hands over her face, as though they were trying to smother her. Thankfully my mother called a local Priest in to bless the house and things seemed to calm down after that. That was the last time I went near a Ouija board, although I knew that there was more and I was intrigued.

I was raised in the Roman Catholic faith. Up until the age of seventeen I was made to go to church every Sunday, including five years serving as an altar boy, but my interest in the paranormal carried on growing. I spent all my spare time in the school library, looking at books about ghosts and the paranormal and I couldn't get enough of it. By the age of nineteen I'd seen several fortune tellers and fell in love with the tarot. I also attended various Spiritualist churches from time to time. By this time I was hooked on getting messages 'from the other side' and this led me to attend meditation and so-called 'personal development' groups. I found a Medium who agreed to teach me how to read tarot cards but I found very quickly that I could read them without being taught. Before long I was doing tarot reading for most of my work colleagues and in many cases it was scary how much private information I seemed to know about their lives. Many of the things I predicted for people came true, although several things never happened.

In my mid-twenties I met my first wife. Even though I'd read her fortune with the tarot cards, she wasn't interested in it in the way that I was and so my spiritual path took a back seat for the next ten years, until the breakdown of my marriage in 2005. For me, 2005 was the most stressful year of my life. At times I would be sitting in my car thinking I just wanted the pain to stop and had even considered taking my own life. However, the thought of knowing how selfish and cruel that would have been to my two young children stopped me from actually going through with it.

One evening at 7pm I found myself sitting on a church bench outside a locked church crying, because I couldn't imagine which way my life was going or where I was going to live. Something had to change, and for me I turned to the church and God for the answers. And I got them. My divorce settlement wasn't as bad as it might have been and I found a place to live that was suitable for when my kids came to stay.

Even though I'd developed a closer relationship with God, my involvement with the occult grew at a massive rate. The house I moved to was only five minutes' drive away from a thriving Spiritualist church and I had no one to hold me back! Over the next couple of years I was drawn deeper into Mediumship and was learning how to contact spirit guides and other spirits. At one point I was doing platform work, where myself and another Medium were invited to different Spiritualist churches, to give messages from the other side.

It was about this time I started to get involved in different healing methods, and it was Reiki healing that I was drawn to the most. I paid a small fortune to get attuned to level one and a short time later I completed my level two. It was during level one that we began inviting other so-called healing spirits into our lives. In my case the healing spirit looked like a monk but I never saw his face. I saw some strange things inside people's bodies while doing Reiki and lots of dark shadows moving around.

Things in my life began to get worse around this time, and in 2008 I hit the next most stressful time in my life. I had little money coming in and had been using my credit cards to live off. Once again, I was crying myself to sleep and asking God to smooth out my path for me. And yet again He answered my prayers by getting the right people in front of me to guide me through my challenges. Not only did I get help with sorting out my financial problems, I found myself wanting to go to church. At this stage I had withdrawn from attending the Spiritualist 'church' as I knew something wasn't right.

I'd always considered myself a Christian (a Christian Spiritualist) but was starting to wonder why some Christians just seemed different to me, as though I was missing something. It was around this time that the Jehovah Witnesses started knocking on my door. We had some very interesting two hour discussions on my doorstep. Though I didn't agree with their view of things, I started dipping into my Bible, just so I could be armed with a solid foundation for our next talk.

At the same time, I visited some Christian websites and forums. This helped me with trying to understand certain parts of the Bible that I hadn't really understood or accepted (due mainly to Spiritualism). But using the internet to research being a Christian is like walking through a minefield; there seemed to be a lot of people that just wanted to condemn me as soon as they found out I was involved in Spiritualism.

I'm an Alarm Engineer and found myself asking my customers about their faith. If they seemed receptive, I would tell them about my spiritual search as I was hungry to know the truth. I had a call to a new customer and we started talking about faith and he mentioned that his daughter, Aliss and her husband, ran a church and café and that there were miracles happening there on a regular basis. It sounded good but just a little far-fetched, although I agreed that he could email her newsletters to me.

The emails I received were short videos of ordinary people being interviewed in a café in Blacon, Chester. They seemed to be claiming all sorts of miracles like broken wrists being healed, hearing being fully restored and lots of other ailments being cured, all as a result of being prayed for. I'd healed people using Reiki but these videos just seemed to knock the socks off anything I did. At first I wondered if maybe they were set up, but there were too many different people and they seemed real, so I decided to see for myself.

Visiting this little café in Blacon became a turning point in my life. I'd tried things my way for so long and didn't seem to be getting anywhere. The first time I went, I had a nice cooked breakfast and was hoping to witness some of these healings in person. I didn't witness any miracles that day, so I decided to give it another try the following week.

It was then that I met Aliss, the café owner. Along with a friend of hers, she came and spoke to me for almost forty minutes and they prophesied over me. I asked a lot of questions about being a Christian (I never said a thing about my connection with Spiritualism) and at the end of the discussion Aliss looked me in the eye and asked, "So, would you like to give your life to Jesus?" I was taken aback and replied, "No, not yet." The truth is, that short question was like being hit with a lightning bolt. I wanted to say yes but was scared. My mind was racing and I didn't understand why.

After talking with Aliss and asking many more questions I found myself wondering if I could really let go of my interest in the occult. For me, my biggest and strongest link to Spiritualism was with my tarot cards that I'd owned for over twenty years. So, one day after work, I decided to get rid of them and destroy them completely; I shredded them! I looked at the last card before dropping it into the shredder and it was the card with the devil controlling two people like puppets and I realized I'd been controlled like that most of my life. I then started clearing all my occult related books and anything else connected with Spiritualism from my shelves and tearing them up and shredding what I could. It was at that point I knew that I'd done the right thing.

The following week, I got down to the café for nine o'clock to speak to Aliss. It turned out she wasn't meant to be there but had just popped in with groceries. When I saw her, I had a huge grin on my face and I said, "Aliss, do you remember the question you asked me last week? Well, if you ask me again, my answer will be very different." We sat down together, I said a prayer and I gave my life to Jesus Christ, and it felt great!

My life has changed so much since then. I've been blessed in so many ways and made many new friends and have even appeared on TV to talk about the dangers of Spiritualism. But for me the biggest blessing God has gifted me with is a wonderful wife whom I met in church and we are now part of the leadership team at our local church. Interestingly I found since I gave my life to Jesus, reading the Bible makes so much more sense and has more meaning than it ever did before. I was baptized in water a few months after giving my life to Jesus and am now "born again."

During a 'School of the Spirit' meeting one Friday night, I was filled with the Holy Spirit for the first time. I was standing with my eyes closed and had a vision. In the front of the room I was seeing a wispy white smoke rising from the floor and forming a cloud about two feet off the ground. I felt that the Lord Jesus was in the middle of the cloud and was blowing the smoke over the whole room. At this stage I was hardly aware of what was going on in the room around me. Someone said something about praying for each other. I was rooted to the spot where I stood and someone prayed. I felt as though I was on fire, there was such an intense heat. I have no idea how long I was standing there but felt I needed to sit down before I fell down.

The moment I sat down the second stage hit me; I thought I was going to cry, then started to laugh and I was shaking and going from hot to cold to hot again. My entire body didn't feel like mine but in all this it was such a happy, joyful feeling. I was like this for a while. The girl I was sitting by was in a similar state to me. I tried standing up when I thought I would be OK. I got to my feet and managed a few steps but had to lean against the wall. I then slid down the wall onto the floor, crawled back to my seat and just carried on laughing. I felt so much joy.

Eventually, I managed to gather myself together enough to walk around but was still feeling slightly spaced out. I got into my car and drove out of the parking lot but had to pull over for ten minutes as I was giggling to myself and had a problem with not being able to feel my hands properly. I eventually made it home and felt like I was floating most of the way there. That's a night I'm not going to forget. But I now know when someone asks if I've been baptized in the Holy Spirit, I can say without any doubt that I have. I pray that you are able to experience what I did.

Soon after I gave my life to Jesus, I decided to get rid of the spirit guides who had been giving me information for a number of years. The day before I met with Rob and Aliss to do this, I felt as though I should fast for twenty-four hours, so I did. Rob and Aliss helped me to pray, I asked God to forgive me for channelling spirit guides and listening to them, I then told the spirit guides to leave me in the name of Jesus. As I did this, I watched them walk away and suddenly turn into horrible demons. I had no idea that's what they were all these years as they hadn't appeared that way to me at all.

How many of you out there wish you could wipe the slate clean with God and start again? Well, the good news is.... you can!"

Why don't you pray this prayer with me right now: "Father God, please forgive me for going my own way and for all the things I've done wrong. (If you've been involved in Spiritualism or Reiki, you could ask Him to forgive you for that). Thank you Jesus for dying on the cross for me and thank you Holy Spirit for raising Jesus from the dead so that I can know you. Jesus, I invite you into my life, come and take over. I tell every evil spirit to leave in the name of Jesus and I invite the Holy Spirit to come in power. Amen."

Unexpected Miracles

Chapter Five
MANDI

Introducing Mandi

People are often stunned when I tell them about Mandi; how she came into our little café in Blacon, Chester and received a dramatic miracle in her life. From a background of anger, violence and addiction, she discovered the unconditional love of God and the love and care of others for the first time in her life.

As you read of Mandi's dramatic transformation, know that what God did for Mandi, He can do for you too.

MANDI'S STORY

My first memory is one of fear. I was playing in the front garden of my home in Chester, UK at the age of two, along with my twin sister. An old lady who lived nearby came to our gate and began shouting out that I should be put in the trash can because I was illegitimate. Menacingly, she lunged at me, trying to grab me so she could put me in the trash. I was so terrified that I grabbed my sister's hand, dragged her into the kitchen pantry and hid. I held my breath so that the old lady wouldn't hear me. Despite hiding, the old woman found me; she grabbed hold of me and roughly picked me up, but I managed to break free and we both hid again.

I was terrified, thinking I was about to be thrown out with the trash. But eventually we heard the old woman leave and we slowly and quietly came out of the cupboard. My sister doesn't remember the incident, but I remember it vividly: it was then that I started biting my nails and would often have nightmares about it, I was so traumatized by the experience.

That incident had a profound impact on my life. However, I think my problems began further back, even before I was born. For some reason, I repeatedly kicked my twin sister when we were together in our mother's womb. She was born black and blue, and as a result, needed to be kept in hospital for three weeks after delivery. I didn't do it on purpose, but my mum took an instant dislike to me and didn't pay me much attention because of it; I felt such guilt.

Looking back, I suspect my mother had what is now termed 'Asperger's syndrome', although it wasn't recognized at the time. She seemed unable to show love and affection to anyone. She was extremely abrupt and everything was black and white. She used to be very violent towards me, and from an early age would hit me with metal dog leads. She grew up in the Royal Air Force in Singapore and then her family came to England.

She met my father when she was twelve. She was crying at a bus stop and he pulled over in his wagon and befriended her. He preyed on the vulnerable and groomed my mother from the age of twelve. By fifteen she was pregnant. She went on to have four children by the time she was nineteen, but my father was married with six other children, so my mum had to bring us up on her own which must have been difficult for her. She would vent all her anger and frustration out on me and I just used to accept all the stress and the anger and the bitterness. It made me feel rotten and worthless with no confidence; I just felt nothing.

When I was eleven, I used to hang around with sixteen-year-old boys. My mother didn't take us out anywhere and there was no stimulation at home – no games or playing, so I would spend time with these boys. They would get high by sniffing glue. I remember one day I was given some glue by one of the boys and I tried it for myself. I would hallucinate about fairground rides and outings and nice things that I didn't have, so I continued sniffing glue regularly for six years.

By the age of seventeen, I knocked about with forty-year-old men and women who were heroin addicts. I'd left home by this time and moved into a communal house with the addicts. It was then that they offered me heroin for the first time. I was excited because they were all doing it. I pulled up my sleeve, they injected me with the heroin and I couldn't believe the feeling of freedom, as though the pain and the worthlessness I had always felt were gone. For the first time ever in my life, I felt good. But because the high was so short-lived, it began a full-blown addiction as I tried to maintain those feelings. Of course, I needed to pay for the heroin and so I made money through prostitution, thieving, burglaries and extorting money from people, all from the age of seventeen.

I also got into alcohol. I was drinking heavily and became an alcoholic which led me to prison. I was angry at my mother and as I was so angry, under the influence of drink it turned to hatred, and then I'd be violent towards the police. I'd be noisy in the street and shouting angrily at people. The police would try to approach me, so I'd beat them up and then I'd get arrested. I've been to prison ten times for hitting the police and other people. In total I've had nearly two hundred convictions for fraud, violence, grievous bodily harm, stealing, breach of the peace, all kinds of things. My family weren't happy; I think they felt helpless and my mum felt a bit guilty and they didn't know what to do with me. I was just in a downward self-destruct mode for many, many years.

I've lived in all kinds of places. I lived in an affluent part of Chester where I was a Madam in a brothel. I had some girls on the game there. One was a doctor's daughter; she spoke the Queen's English and was very popular. Running the brothel helped pay for my drugs. I've lived in crack houses - filthy, grotty hovels. Some have been very posh places and I had the money to pay for them, but I moved around a lot because my behavior would get me kicked out. I'd often be evicted due to noisy parties, so I would need to keep moving around. I also got into a lot of debt, and rather than have people catch up with me, I'd move on to a new place.

I've only ever had two proper jobs. One was as a Care Assistant in a nursing home. It was a Christian nursing home and I spent twelve months there, but I was drinking heavily and it was affecting my work so I had to leave. My other job was on a farm. One day, I was sent to count the cows because there were poachers around and the farmer wanted to make sure they were all still there. After counting, I went back in and said, "There are forty cows and one's asleep." The farmer replied, "What do you mean, 'one's asleep'?" I said, "I mean it's on its back with its legs in the air." It had been shot by the poachers. It still makes me chuckle now when I think of it.

Another time, the farmer asked me to take an electric fence down from one side of the field, but I took the wrong fence down and the cattle got into the other field and mated with a different breed. Then I had to bring the cows down from one field and into the farm. This meant crossing over a main road, but unfortunately a fire truck came through with its sirens blaring. It so startled the cows that they scarpered everywhere and crushed the neighbor's rose bushes and nice garden. As you can imagine, I didn't last long in that job!

One time, I'd run amok with a knife in the street trying to attack everyone. The police put me in a hospital wing of a remand center. A prominent psychiatrist came to see me and he put me in Denbigh hospital on a lock-up ward where I had a drug induced psychosis: a nervous breakdown and schizophrenic breakdown all at the same time. I completely lost my mind. The devil got on top of me and I was hearing voices from the radio and news bulletins all talking about me, but it was all just in my head. I was there for twelve months. I was kicked out of there in the end for bad behavior, but luckily the probation service didn't believe I was kicked out of hospital so they let me off the charges and I didn't have to go back to court.

At this point, I was taking four bags of heroin a day and I was on about $300 worth of crack every day which I funded through prostitution and burglary.

One day, I went to my drug dealer's house down the street in Blacon, Chester. She wasn't in and I was desperate for speed because I was hooked on speed as well, and I was cursing her because she wasn't in. I went and sat on the wall opposite the shops and it was pouring with rain. I didn't know what to do, but suddenly I heard a voice in my head repeatedly say, "Go to the café, go to the café" and I thought, "I'm not going to the café, I'll miss my drug dealer." I didn't even know there was a café there, but the voice was persistent and as I looked up I noticed a café sign outside a strange looking building right in front of me. As I was soaking wet, cold and hungry I thought I'd just go to the café, grab a bite to eat and be quick so I could go to the dealer's again.

I walked into the café and spotted an addict I knew, so I asked him for some drugs. "Hiya Mandi," he said, "I don't have any drugs; Jesus is my habit now." I said, "Oh yeah?" and he replied, "Yeah, do you want Jesus? Do you want some prayer?" So I went "Yeaaaah, just give me whatever you've got, give me some Jesus." He asked Sarah to pray for me, so she came over and began to pray.

Suddenly, something dramatic happened. All the bitterness and anger and hurt and worthlessness and every negative emotion I'd felt in my life came to the forefront as she was praying for me and I just burst into tears, sobbing uncontrollably. The café was packed but I didn't care who heard. I was oblivious to everyone else. I was aware of the Holy Spirit coming into my life as Sarah prayed and I felt such an inner peace: 'all loved up'. I became completely calm and relaxed and all the pain ebbed away. I still get emotional now just thinking about it, but it was such a wonderful feeling. I just felt the feeling of love from God. I knew it was from God the Holy Spirit, I knew that God had entered my life and was healing me. I wanted Jesus to come in so I asked Him to.

Needless to say, after that experience I didn't go back to the dealer's. In fact, I came off all the alcohol and drugs straight away. I did it cold turkey and I started going to the café every morning at nine o'clock from that day on, spending the whole day there. I was living in a flat nearby but didn't even have a bed. It was so dirty and the front door had a huge hole kicked in. The new friends I made at the café and church really cared for me. I'd never known that kind of love before. They cleaned and decorated my flat, bought me some furniture and fixed the front door. But the drug dealers started to come and offer me free drugs to try and get me back on the stuff, and friends on the run from the police wanted to stay. I was a bit of a pushover, so I knew I had to move out.

I tried to find some help and a place to live, but no-one in the whole of the country would take me because of my reputation for violence, stealing and preying on the vulnerable. Nowhere would give me a bed: no homeless hostels, no halfway houses, no women's refuges or rehab centers. As soon as they heard who I was and saw my police record they all refused me point blank. Sarah spent a long time and tried everywhere for me.

I had also suffered from schizophrenia in the past, but after I gave my life to Jesus, the evil spirit of schizophrenia left me when we told it to go at a School of the Spirit meeting. Not only did I feel it leave, but I saw it go. It looked like a big monkey sitting on my back and then it disappeared. I knew it was connected to the drugs. Because of all this on my record, no-one would take me, but I had to leave my flat urgently.

God then showed Sarah that she should offer me a place in her home, so I moved in there. Sarah would pray with me through the night as I came off methadone, heroin, speed, crack, valium, tama-zepam and alcohol. It got easier and easier as each night went on. I just felt that I was doing the right thing for God and that God wanted me to do this and that He wanted me. I'd never been wanted by anyone before. Sarah was teaching me about how God loved me and how He had a plan for me and it was very encouraging, like she was giving me a hope for the future.

One day when it was particularly tough, we decided to read the Bible together in my room. I was craving crack and I was feeling angry and Sarah suggested that I read the Scripture for a change. Usually she was the one reading it to me. So I agreed and as I was reading the Bible out loud, all of a sudden this cloud of white smoke came off Sarah's left shoulder and rose right up into the air. I shouted, "What's that!?" I jumped up and started patting her back saying "Sarah, Sarah!" and she thought she had a huge spider on her back. I said, "You're on fire, you're on fire!" It turned out to be the presence of the Holy Spirit, letting me know He was with us through this situation. The calm and the love we felt was just amazing. After that experience, all the drugs and addictions just went out the window.

I had a probation officer whom I met with regularly. I told her about the café and how going there had changed my life, so she came with me for a coffee and to see where all the miracles were happening that she'd heard about. She had a bad arm, so Sarah prayed for her arm and she felt tingling and warmth all up her arm and it got healed instantly! My psychiatric nurse couldn't believe the change in me. It's unexplainable naturally speaking, because I was a psychotic wreck but suddenly I was level headed, sensible and respectable and people just couldn't believe the change in me.

An off-duty police woman at Aliss and Rob's church watched as I gave my testimony one day. I explained who I was and how Jesus had changed my life. This police officer knew the old me. But she had no idea I was the same woman: I'd changed so much in such a short space of time. When we got chatting, she told me that one time when I was drinking, she was the officer who had arrested me five times in one week. I didn't know it then, but she was a Christian and prayed for me. She thanked God that her prayer had been answered and that I'd found Jesus. She couldn't believe the change in me and hadn't even recognized me. It was only when she heard my name that she realized who I was.

My family moved away from Chester and moved to the other end of the country to get away from me because they'd had enough of me and the trouble I was in. But now I'm clean and like a different person, they've had me over to stay and we're building bridges now. I do love my mum despite what she's been like and she loves me despite what I've been like and we've both forgiven each other, so we're moving forward.

I grew up thinking I was a lesbian, but somehow I

never felt comfortable with it and since I've met Jesus I'm no longer lesbian and I like men. I don't feel guilty any more: it's like my sins were scarlet and now they're gone and I'm white as snow. I can hold my head high and be happy in myself since I met Jesus.

I used to be a bag of bones and gaunt, grey and unkempt. I didn't wash and my flat was a mess. Now I'm like a new person and people comment on how I seem to glow and radiate Jesus. Jesus is wonderful: He's given me a new life and I'm grasping it. I feel respectable now; I respect myself, I love myself because God loves me. I've met beautiful people. When you're an addict you're around people who are selfish and they steal from you and they beat you up and rape you and all kinds of nasty horrible things. They were out of control as well as I was, so it was total chaos, but the life I have now is so calm and full of peace.

God is restoring my mind and everything is becoming normal. I've had slurred speech because of all the substance misuse and my concentration and memory were not good, but Jesus is restoring that daily and my future is with Jesus.

As you read my story, I pray that you will know God. Give your life to Jesus; hand your life over and let Jesus heal you and He will. He will heal your heart. Ask Him to forgive all your sin and He will help you to forgive others. That will bring a huge release for you, just like it did for me.

Never give up because God's always there right behind you. Maybe you've made some bad choices, but God's right there ready to grasp your hand and take you to a better future. There are fellow Christians who can help you and support you through difficult times. Never give up hope because Jesus is there waiting for you. Just ask Him.

Pray with Aliss:

"Heavenly Father, thank you for your forgiveness. I choose to forgive........ for all the ways they hurt me, just as you have forgiven me. Lord Jesus, thank you that you are patient with me and I ask you to help me now. I tell any spirit of rejection, fear, hatred and addiction to leave in the name of Jesus. By faith I receive your freedom, your love and your peace in my heart. Amen."

Chapter Six
TIM
Introducing Tim

I watched as Tim arrived at our workshop in Houston, Texas. For thirty-three years he had no feeling in almost his entire body, he had brain damage, loss of hearing, poor eyesight and tremors. My heart went out to him when I heard he was unable to write his name legibly as he signed into our event.

We've witnessed many dramatic miracles at our workshops, but his story so touched me that I interviewed him about his life so you could hear his remarkable story. You will be moved as you read of the tragic accident which left him disabled as a young man. But what happened next changed his life. If you need a miracle, ask the Lord Jesus to do the same for you.

TIM'S STORY

I was born and raised in Texas, USA. My family consisted of me, my parents and older brother and we were all Catholic. My brother and I never got on. He seemed to hate me and many times I thought he was going to kill me. When I was thirteen and my brother fifteen, my dad had 156 loads of dirt delivered to our home and dad made us work it down into our one-acre plot. It was a low lying area and my dad wanted to build it up, so throughout the blistering summer heat, me and my brother had to dig it all in.

It was back breaking work. One day my brother had finally had enough of it all and was angry with dad. He said, "I'm gonna kill him." He seemed to be serious, so I questioned him: "You're really gonna kill dad?" All I remember next is falling forward towards the ground and a pain in my head. Stunned, I tried to pick myself up, but before I could work out what just happened - boom, there came another blow to the back of my head and down I went again. My brother was hitting me with his shovel, trying to kill me.

I managed to get away and staggered into the house feeling sick. All I wanted to do was take a shower and cool off. I ran the shower, stepped under the water and felt searing pain. All around I saw streams of bright red blood that was pouring from the back of my head. I dried off, went and found dad and told him I needed to take the rest of the day off. I lay down on my bed for a while until I felt better. A few days later my mom discovered my pillow case covered with blood and wanted to know what had happened. But I was unable to tell her much as I couldn't recall all the details. I still have two scars on the back of my head from that incident, and plenty more from where my brother attacked me at other times. My childhood wasn't the happiest.

When I was sixteen years old, my aunt became a 'born again' believer in Jesus. We happened to be at her house one day for a barbecue and she asked if I wanted to give my life to God. I said, "Well of course I do!" I didn't know exactly what I was doing but I wanted to make sure that me and God were on good terms. The following year I was baptized in a pond and then a month later I was baptized with the Holy Spirit. I still remember when that happened; it felt like a nuclear bomb going off inside of me and I loved it!

It seemed that I was rebelling against the traditional Catholic church of which my family were members. Their church reminded me of the Pharisees in Jesus' day. But I thought that if I'd been living in those times, I would have been hanging out with John the Baptist, not the religious Pharisees. My aunt was pleased that I had chosen to follow Jesus and she also led my cousins and her husband (my uncle) to Jesus too. But my parents weren't so happy. They were full-on traditional Catholics and didn't like the fact that I was 'born again.' They didn't appreciate the Holy Spirit as much as I did.

Things changed when I gave my life to Jesus at sixteen. I was much happier: I didn't fear death like I had before, and other fears left too. It was wonderful. I had love overflowing, coming out of me, but my parents thought there was something wrong with me. They knew I wasn't on drugs or drinking alcohol, but they couldn't work out why I was so happy and loving and praising God. So my dad decided to take me to see the Catholic Priest who wanted me to attend the church conversion classes. I told the Priest that since I'd been going to that church all my life, I didn't need to be converted. He said my actions weren't what you'd consider to be normal and asked if I was on drugs. I told him I could come to his conversion class, but I'd end up having more converts to Jesus than he would to his church. He wasn't amused. Finally, the Priest said to my dad, "If it was my kid, I'd kick him out of the house." My dad seemed to hate me. He wanted me to become a Catholic Priest, but it became obvious when I gave my life to Jesus and became full of the Holy Spirit that that wasn't going to happen. From that time, I felt the full force of his hatred and disapproval.

I was good friends with a girl at school whom I liked a lot. I was hoping we would become more than just friends. We were very close, and I had that feeling you get when you're first in love. We spent a lot of time together in eleventh grade and everything seemed to be falling into place. I knew I wanted to spend the rest of my life with her. But I never got chance. All my hopes and dreams for a life with her were shattered when she was suddenly taken from me; she was killed in a car accident at the age of seventeen. That tore me up, but nobody offered me any help or condolence. I tried to push the sense of loss and heartache away and didn't care about much after that.

Soon after, I graduated High School. Most kids receive a gift from their parents when they graduate – some even a car. When I graduated my dad told me he'd got my gift in the driveway. I was excited, thinking perhaps it could be a new vehicle. But as we got out into the driveway, he turned to me and bluntly demanded: "I want you to get out of my house." My heart sank. I dutifully went inside to my room and started to pack my clothes. My mom couldn't understand what was happening and was distressed by it all. But I went over to my cousins' house and stayed with them for a while.

I had no skills and didn't know what to do when I got out of High School, so I decided to join the army. I wanted to get away from everything and signed up for three years, aged eighteen. I thought if I joined the army there was a chance I may die, but I didn't really care; I would be with the girl I loved.

After training, I was posted to Fort Knox, Kentucky. I wasn't keen on the idea of just sitting around and guarding gold, but that's mainly what we did. I attended a local church and got engaged during that time to a girl whom I would later marry.

I was a driver for the Lieutenant of my company and took care of the jeep and track vehicles and I kept the guns clean. After I'd been there for around one year, my Lieutenant told us about a Brigade Show nearby that was coming up. He wanted to put the tanks on display there and he put me in charge of getting four of the vehicles ready for the Show. The first was an M113A troop transporter where all the Captains were given intelligence from the Major and Colonel. It had maps, radios, and a lot more space than the second vehicle; a command track. Then there was a Bradley plus an M1 Abrams tank from the 1960s. A lot of work was needed to get them up to standard. We had to sandblast each vehicle, repaint them, add new stickers and generally make them look good. I worked on that job for three months.

Finally, the day arrived for the Brigade Show. We were all apprehensive as everything needed to be up to scratch and working perfectly. I was also responsible for getting them to the Show on time. We arrived in the building where the vehicles were stored and discovered to our dismay that the Communications Sergeant who tested all the vehicle radios the previous night, had left the power on. This meant that the large military radios in the vehicles had consumed all the power of each tank overnight. We had four big batteries in each of the vehicles, but they were all dead. We had just forty-five minutes to get the vehicles down to the Brigade Show four miles away, but nothing was working.

As our minds were racing, one of the drivers spotted a huge generator in the corner of the building and told me he knew how to operate it. It would normally take a big army truck to pull it, but we got three of the guys to push it over to the four vehicles. The young private cranked up the generator and managed to get it going. He knew how to operate it but unfortunately, what he didn't seem to know, was that a 300-amp 24 vault diesel generator produces a lot of energy and needs to be earthed. Not grounding it was a bad decision.

Oblivious to this, we found the right connection for the tanks. I jumped into the first vehicle, plugged it in and had the power working. I turned the master switch and was relieved when it started first time. I then got into the second vehicle and started that in the same way. With the third vehicle I did the same: everything lit up ready to start, I put my right hand on the periscope cover as I had done with the others and I pushed the button. As I did so, my colleagues witnessed what seemed to be bright lightning flashing out of the vehicle and knew something was terribly wrong. Without even thinking to turn off the generator, they raced over to where I was.

All I remember is that when I hit that button, I experienced the worst shock I could ever imagine. Electricity surged through my body causing immense pain and I saw blue arcs shooting out of each finger of my right hand, the sort a welder might see. I then blacked out.

Four hours later, I woke up in a military hospital bed hooked up to monitors. A nurse stood over me as I came to. "He's waking up" she shouted as she ran to fetch the doctor. My body was burning. It felt on fire. A copper metal taste was in my mouth. The military doctor arrived and exclaimed, "What are you doing alive? You should be dead." I asked him what had happened. All I could think was that I had to get to the Brigade Show. "I've only got forty-five minutes to get the vehicles down there, I need to go!" I blurted out. "Son, that Show's over," was his calm reply. I felt I'd let everyone down. I had the responsibility to get the vehicles to the Show and opened up to the public. I really didn't remember anything about the accident. Both my body and my mind had been badly affected.

The doctor told me I'd been electrocuted. "Do you know anything about electricity?" he asked. "No, I don't" I replied. "Except I don't like it." Thoughts of jail raced through my mind, but he told me to calm down, I wouldn't be going to jail and that I'd been hurt in the line of duty. They tested my blood, but I had nothing out of the ordinary in my system because I didn't drink or do drugs. He advised me to rest up and they kept me in the hospital for twenty-two hours while they carried out tests. The nurse poked me with a needle all over, but I couldn't tell the difference between that and the pain caused by the electrocution. It felt like my whole body was being jabbed with red hot needles constantly!

It seemed as though my whole body was on fire, apart from the thumb and forefinger of my right hand. From my head to my toes, I was in pain. When they asked how the pain was, I told them sarcastically, "Oh it's great" and they thought I meant it, so they only gave me an aspirin. I looked the same as usual, but I smelled so bad of burning and felt like I was on fire.

The following day I was discharged from hospital and foolishly I went straight back to my company and back into work. There were no physical wounds or external injuries, and so everyone thought I was okay. I naively assumed that the pain would leave over the next few hours and I would be back to normal. I didn't realize the full extent of the damage initially, but as the days progressed, it became clear to me just how badly I'd been injured.

Back to work and the first morning I didn't hear my alarm, so I overslept. People were pounding on my door and I didn't hear them either. Everything seemed really muffled; my hearing was wrecked, and my taste had gone. All I could taste was copper metal. My mind wasn't in the right place either. At the end of that first day's work, we gathered together in formation for the top Sergeant to tell us the plans for the following day. We were dismissed and everyone else went home. But two hours later, I was still standing there. My mind was all messed up. I didn't know what I was doing. My Commander came out after I had been standing there for two hours, after everyone had eaten, and I was still in formation. It had rained while I was standing there, but I hadn't even noticed. I hadn't eaten. I couldn't put anything together. So he took me off and assigned me a room-mate to look after me. I bunked together with him and he watched out for me, but that was a difficult time for both of us.

It took three or four months before I could hold myself together, but the accident left my brain irreparably damaged. Eventually the copper metal taste disappeared and the burning pain left some months later. It was then that I discovered my body was numb. Apart from my right thumb and forefinger, I had no feeling in my body whatsoever.

I kept working, even though my mind and my body were messed up. I was posted to Germany in August of that year for eighteen months and I carried on working, trying to make sense of why I had enlisted in the army; I couldn't even remember. It was there that the tremors in my body began. I didn't have control over my body like I used to before the accident, and the more I tried to force my brain to function right, the more my hands shook. They shook constantly. I would break things as I reached for them, costing me money to replace them. I thought it was so unfair as none of it was my fault.

I gave up writing because no-one could read what I had written. I couldn't even write my name; my hands shook so much. I also found reading difficult and couldn't seem to do that either after the accident. Things got pretty bad as I kept attempting to do the things I'd done before. I was still only a kid. I remember in Germany we were playing American football and I got clipped by a guy who was mad at me, probably due to my lack of coordination as I couldn't feel anything or hear properly. I got concussion and that only added to my problems. The ambulance driver held up his fingers and I was seeing double. My Corporal pulled an engagement photo of my fiancée and me from my wallet and showed it me. I recognized my fiancée, but I had no idea who the guy next to her was; I was that concussed! My Captain came to see me that night and I said, "I know you, don't I?" He asked if I recognized who he was and I replied to his face, "Yeah, you're that stupid guy in charge of all of us, that can't do nothin' right." That was totally not me.

I worked out in the gym every day trying to get my muscles to work properly but I had no feeling in my body, so it was difficult. Apart from the thumb and forefinger of my right hand, if I touched any surface, I couldn't feel it. Walking was difficult because I couldn't feel my legs or my feet. I had to concentrate on the ground and place my feet down carefully. Sometimes one of my legs would go out and I didn't seem to have control over it and I often fell.

I came out of the army, got married and had four beautiful children. A month after our wedding, my brother was in a serious accident which destroyed his life. His friend fell asleep at the wheel of his sports car, they crossed over the median, entered the other lane and a station wagon smashed into the side of their car. My brother used to make fun of people with disabilities and call them names. I would be so embarrassed and tell him off, but what was strange is that everything he made fun of before his accident, he became. He ended up in a wheel-chair in a nursing home.

When I came out of the army, I got a job as an auto mechanic, then a truck driver and then trained as a nurse. I somehow managed to work even with the tremors and with no feeling in my body. The tremors caused my hands to shake so badly that I couldn't drink coffee without spilling it everywhere; it looked like I'd taken a bath! I overcame this problem by using a special mug with a lid and small opening so I could drink it. Over the years I broke many glasses and bottles just trying to take a drink. I often cut my hand because I couldn't tell how much pressure I was applying and would grip a glass too tightly. If someone came up behind me and tapped me on the shoulder I wouldn't know, they had to push me forward. I even had people come up behind and cut me with a knife to see if I could tell, but I couldn't feel it. I tore my hand apart on a fence once. Another time I ran down the stairs and ripped my hand on a nail in the wall. It took me a while to adjust to the changes in my body and my mind after the accident.

Sadly, things didn't work out with my wife and we got divorced. That's when I turned away from God. My life was bad. I moved back down to Houston when I was thirty-two, to take care of my brother and my mother (who was no longer with my father). My mom was extremely frail. My brother was six foot four and a big guy, although now in a wheelchair. One day my mom fell and broke her hip. I had to get my brother out of his wheelchair, put him in the car and go down to the hospital with my mother. All this with shaking hands and a numb body! My mother underwent surgery to screw her femur back together, then remained in hospital for a month of therapy.

The day I brought her home, she requested her favorite meal: seafood gumbo. I bought the fish, shrimp and oysters and lovingly made it for her. She told me it was the best gumbo she'd tasted. My brother finished his and tried to make a joke while I was putting the leftovers away. He then decided to transfer to his wheelchair from the wrong direction which meant that he fell and broke his hip too! So back to hospital with him, the same day my mom got out. Then after he was in hospital for thirty days and ready to come out, my mom found out the screws that were put into her femur had killed the nerve which caused the bone to die. So she had to go back in when my brother came out. I was the only one to look after them. It was a stressful time and that's when I started smoking cigarettes. I was my mom's carer for seventeen years until she died.

I was away from the Lord for twenty-five years. Thankfully, He never let me go; I was the one running away. I blamed Him for my disastrous marriage and for my poor relationship with my kids. However, despite this, I was able to find love with a long-lost friend. I've known Judy since the week I was born. We lost touch for years but met up again and now we're happily married.

My cousin discovered he was Jewish, and after researching it, we both got heavily into Judaism. It seemed a bit like Catholicism to me, but we got into the Torah, the law, and we debated with Christians. I saw Christianity as evil. I stopped going to church and observed the Jewish traditions instead.

But one day, I came across Aliss on 'It's Supernatural' TV show with Sid Roth. I bought her 'Normal Supernatural Christian' book and CD set and I listened to her CDs over and over until they almost wore out. I started to get jealous. I couldn't understand why God had given her a gift of healing. This caused me to search out the Scriptures in the New Testament and I discovered how the Old Testament, the Jewish Scriptures, point to Jesus.

I purposed in my heart that if Aliss ever came to the States, I would go so she could teach me how to bring healing to others. It never crossed my mind to want healing for myself. I saved up so I could travel to see her when she came. It was ironic, but I had an operation running in my back shed where I made illegal moonshine. I was listening to Aliss' CDs at the same time as I made the moonshine. One day I was trying to get the lid off a barrel that held the mash and I hit my good thumb so hard it bent my fingernail all the way up, so it was standing at a ninety-degree angle to my thumb. I had tears coming out of my eyes with the pain. I remembered Aliss saying "Just tell the pain to go away in Jesus' name." So I did, and as soon as I said the words, the pain was gone.

Immediately some Scriptures from the New Testament came to mind: "I am with you until the end of the age," "I will never leave you nor forsake you" and more. Here I was, doing something illegal, and I knew God was there and speaking to me. That convicted me. I pleaded, "God I can't do this anymore." I'd had enough of trying to live my life without Him.

I then discovered that not only was Aliss going to be in the States, but she was coming to my city of Houston, Texas on 22 June that year, 2018. "Oh my gosh," I thought, "I'm not going to miss this! I'm gonna see this girl and find out about the favor she has with God."

The night before the workshop I had a dream. I was in Jerusalem at the time of Jesus. I saw Jesus walking about seventy-five feet from me and a guy with black shoulder length hair approached me and asked, "Would you like to meet Jesus?" "Yes" I replied. "Matter of fact" he went on, "You'd like to be healed, wouldn't you?" "I would love to be healed" I gasped. He grabbed my arm and dragged me through a tight knit crowd of people. No one could get through, but we got through. He told me to reach out and touch His hem. I reached out and Jesus looked down at me. He said, "You're healed, be on your way." Then I woke up. It makes me cry just thinking about it now. I hadn't had a dream like that for a very long time.

Excitedly, I travelled to the workshop. I knew it was the sabbath, which I'd been observing with the Jewish faith, but it didn't stop me. A guy there asked what I came for. I said, "Dude, I'm gonna get my healing." I had no idea how it was going to happen. I didn't even know what I was going to be healed from; I couldn't think straight. My brain was still damaged from the accident.

During the first session on miracles, Aliss talked about Jesus and His love. She demonstrated a miracle through the power of Jesus and a lady gave her life to the Lord. She then got us all to pair up and give it a try for ourselves. A guy walked towards me, but a younger guy came over and said, "No I've got this one." I didn't care who prayed. Jon began to pray for me and as he did, I felt something like an innertube full of power surround my head; I knew it was the Holy Spirit. I felt such peace. I noticed something happening to my mind, I can't describe the feeling, but I knew it was being fixed. The 'innertube' moved down around my entire body and wherever it moved, the feeling came back. I could feel the clothes on my back, the breeze of the air conditioning, even people's breath – Jon blew the Holy Spirit on me, and the power went all the way down to my feet; I was healed.

After thirty-three years of disability since the accident, I got all the feeling back in my body. All the numbness left instantly. Over the lunch break I went outside. The hot sun on the door handle made me jump as I grabbed it, I wasn't used to the feeling. I took my shoes and socks off and slid my bare feet over the grass. What a wonderful feeling. I no longer had to look down as I walked. I got a pen and some paper and wrote my name perfectly. I wrote a whole paragraph and was showing everyone. I was elated. I had got my healing; Jesus had healed me.

The afternoon sessions were like a blur to me, and at the evening meeting there were many miracles and families giving their lives to Jesus. During the meeting, Aliss called out and asked if I was there. She'd heard about my healing. I raised my hand and went up to the front. My brain felt like liquid. It was so strange. I shared about the miracle and people could see that my hands were not shaking. We were all rejoicing and shouting praises to God. As Aliss did so, something strange happened. My hearing went and I couldn't hear anything at all; it was even worse than before. I was puzzled as I didn't know what was happening. But then, in an instant, all my hearing was fully restored perfectly. I also stopped smoking that day.

My brain functioned much better after the workshop, and after about six months it was fully back to normal. Since my healing, I think differently. I don't think like I used to; it's much better. I thank God that everything has been restored. Near the end of the workshop, Aliss said God was giving people inventions and you know what? He gave me a couple of inventions that day which I've been working on. I'm also writing a book. To think, I couldn't even read or write for the past thirty-three years! My life hasn't been the same since that day.

I went back to see my doctor the week after my healing. Not only had my hearing, tremors, brain and numbness been healed, but I found that I had also been healed of diabetes. Since 1998 I had been diabetic type 2, but when my doctor tested me after the workshop, my blood sugar level had gone right down and was borderline, which means the levels are no longer in the diabetes range. He sent me to the optometrist to check my eyes. Previously, there had been problems, but no trace of diabetic retinopathy existed. My eyesight had tested 20/40 in one eye and 20/25 in the other. After my healing, my eyes were 20/25 and 20/20 which is amazing. I was told I no longer need to go to the diabetic clinic. God is so good.

My neighbor was crippled because of crystallization and calcification on his knees. Both knees were bad and he spent most of his time indoors as a result. I visited him after the workshop and told him about my miracle. He said he was ready to be healed too, so I prayed for him. He was in his chair and started crying because all the pain in his knees went away. Now he's hardly ever home; he's got a new lease of life. He has x-rays from before the healing and then a month after I prayed, he went back to the doctor who had to agree it was a miracle. They compared both x-rays and it was obvious that the knees were totally clear of the problem and it looked like cartilage was supernaturally growing back too.

My daughter was diagnosed with cancer. She had a fibrous tumor around her ovary. After the workshop, I kept demanding it to come out of her and the cancer literally came out of her body; she saw it. So many things have been happening. I prayed for a woman in Walgreens and her back got healed and another neighbor wants to give her life to God because I've been telling her about Jesus.

I'm now following Jesus with all my heart. I've been attending the church where the workshop was held and we have seen spectacular miracles there too. We had two shoulder rotator cuffs healed and prayed for a guy who had no hearing since birth. God opened up his ears and he was instantly healed in the parking lot. It's just amazing. God is real and He is good.

Note from Aliss:

Everywhere I've shared Tim's story people are being healed of similar symptoms. A lovely lady who had difficulty walking and severe tremors as a result of a stroke was instantly healed. A guy just out of jail with stenosis in his neck and numb arms and hands was healed and all feeling came back. A woman with Multiple Sclerosis began to walk unaided and then went up the stairs on her own. A lady with Reinhardt's Disease and white, numb hands got all feeling back and the normal color returned instantly.

If you need healing in your body or your mind, receive it now. Take a deep breath in of the Holy Spirit and breathe out all your anxieties, all your anger, your frustration, bitterness, hopelessness or resentment. I release healing through the mighty name of Jesus for you as you read this. You can tell the symptoms and the condition to leave your body in the name of Jesus. Receive your healing now in Jesus' name, Amen.

Chapter Seven
KAMRAN

Introducing Kamran

I first got to know Kamran when he and his wife Suzy came to Chester and visited our Blacon café in 2010. Since then, we've become good friends; they've been back to Chester a number of times and we've stayed at their home in the mountains of North Carolina.

Read Kamran's story of a Muslim boy hungry for a relationship with God and discover the extraordinary way in which the Living God of Love responded.

KAMRAN'S STORY

My name in Farsi, my first language is pronounced 'Kom-ron.' I was born in 1967 into a Shia Muslim family in a small city in Iran. Growing up, all I ever wanted was to become a friend of God. I wanted to get to know God, so I became really interested in the religion of Islam. There was no internet in those days and since my mother was a practicing Muslim, I would ask her questions about God. She encouraged me and my brother to do our prayers five times each day and be good Muslim boys. She told us all about the Muslim God and the prophet Mohammad. She taught us to be kind to other people. My father was religious when he was younger, but because he wanted a relationship with God and it never happened, he became discouraged and was no longer a practicing Muslim.

I grew up during the revolution in Iran. At school it was a hot topic, a stew pot for all things Islamic. I couldn't imagine anything but Islam. From a young age, I had a burning desire deep in my heart, at the center of my being, to become a close friend of the God I was introduced to.

My father owned a grocery store in the center of our town at the intersection, and I remember one day when I was twelve going to my grandmother's house close by. On the way, I went into a book store and leafed through some Islamic books that were for sale. I picked up a book on wisdom and began to read. It was a softer heart of Islam and talked of helping the poor and needy. I was so drawn to that book because my nature and the cry of my heart was to help the poor and needy. That was the beginning of my journey.

I had a dream about God and angels which also got my attention and I became an avid seeker of God. From a young age, I constantly felt a call in my heart to become a friend of God. During the war in Iran groceries were scarce and the religious leaders often came to our supermarket which stocked almost everything they needed. I asked them, "How do you become a friend of God? How can I get closer to Him?" But nobody had any answers. They told me whatever they knew, but deep down inside I knew there was something more. My biggest desire was to walk with God, but it was not offered through our religion. I did more practicing: praying five times a day and being nice to the poor.

It was a confusing time for me. I was searching and seeking to know God but despite there being plenty of Islamic teaching, no-one was able to share with me anything from their own experience with God. To me, experience meant so much. I sat in the store, helped the customers and tried to be a good

Muslim boy. For years and years I would sit for hours watching the door and waiting. "Surely," I thought, "One day a man will walk in who knows God personally and will share his experiences with me." But that day never came.

When I was eighteen, my dream was to go to war. I didn't want to kill anybody but I wanted to get killed so that I may see God. I was not interested in going to heaven for pleasure, or to escape hell. I would pray, "God, the reason I want to come to heaven is because of you. I love you." Thankfully I did not go to war. However, my father was injured in a bad car accident and for years was in and out of hospitals. I had to take care of the supermarket with my brother. But the desire to get close to God was like a clock and it was ticking and ticking and would never stop ticking. I could not stop thinking about God, for even one moment.

I had a religion, but it was all I had. In my heart I knew there was something more and I knew one day I would become a friend of God. I had been consumed by this desire since I was twelve and by the time I was twenty-seven, I became angry and spiritually bitter because that had not happened. One day in my father's supermarket I looked up. "God, I'm going to stop praying to you and trying to have a relationship with you. I'm going to stop pursuing you. My pursuit is done. I don't want you anymore. Everything between us is done." My heart was broken and I was very confused.

At thirty, I was disappointed and bitter. I became tired of the country and wanted to move to America. My aunt was living in the United States and in 1996 she agreed I could go and stay with her. However, it was difficult for an Iranian, or anyone from the Middle East to enter the USA. Only a very small percentage of people were accepted, and it was unlikely that I would be. If you were one of the few to be accepted for a visa, you needed to wait up to forty days to receive it. I went to a travel agent and told them what I wanted to do. One thing led to another and I ended up in Cyprus with an appointment for the US embassy there. I was a thirty year old Muslim man with a broken heart. I wanted to run away, forget about God, about Islam and religion and start a new life in the USA. I found myself in the lobby of a hotel in Cyprus the day before my embassy appointment. I noticed a Christian Bible on a glass shelf and as I approached I saw that it was written in my language of Farsi. Something made me pick it up.

I had been taught that the Bible was corrupted by Christians and that God had to send a new book, the one read by Muslims. It had made sense to me at the time. But because I was at the end of myself in Cyprus, when I saw that Bible, somehow something inside me was pulling me towards it. In our country it was illegal to have a Bible, so I had no access to one before. I talked to the hotel clerk who could speak some Farsi and asked him if I could read it. He agreed, he gave it to me and I excitedly carried it back to my room. It did not occur to me at the time to ask myself why there was a Farsi speaking clerk and a Farsi Bible in a hotel in a Greek speaking country!

Sitting on the floor, I opened the Bible up at the book of Matthew in the New Testament. "This book and the story of the prophet Jesus is so sweet," I mused to myself. Prior to that day, no writing had tasted so sweet as that Bible. The story made sense to me. It didn't seem to be a religious book, but one that I was drawn to and enjoyed. After a while, each time I read 'Jesus Christ' (Īsā Masīh in Farsi) in the text, the ink with His name would jump up out of the book, come up to my eye level, then up to the ceiling. My gaze followed and I watched His name come down and land back in the book. I didn't think of it as miraculous. I wasn't even wondering if I was having a dream or a vision, I was just reading.

That happened three or four times. The last time His name came out and went to the ceiling, I looked up and there was the Lord Jesus. I didn't call Him that, I just thought He was a prophet. My whole body knew it was Him. The ceiling expanded, Jesus looked down and looked me in the eyes. In Farsi He said, "I will help you get to the United States." I thought in my heart, "Can I pray to this Jesus? He is a prophet to Christians and I am a Muslim." I looked up and said, "Jesus, all the other prophets (and I named them), they never helped me. If you can, please do."

I continued reading as though nothing had happened. However, when I went to the embassy the next day I remembered. I prayed in my heart, "Jesus, you promised that you would help me today. Please help me." Incredibly, I got my visa that day. They stamped my passport and I was so happy. I went back to Iran, packed my bags and arrived at my aunt and uncle's in Atlanta.

I didn't give Jesus the credit for helping me with the visa. Instead I thanked the Muslim God: "It looks like you finally did something and paid some attention to me. You brought me here and sent this Jesus to help me." I still didn't understand why Jesus showed up, but no other prophet came to help me.

When I arrived in the US, my heart was broken. I was done with religion, so I decided I was going to start living. I thought perhaps Hollywood was waiting for me and I could become a model or an actor, even though I couldn't speak English. I had all these big dreams and I'd seen the movies, but then I ended up working for a marble company, run by beautiful Muslim people who were also Iranian. We would cut the marble countertops and polish them. I was also working for a vending machine company. I was earning just $7 per hour and I thought, "I've come all the way to the United States just for this?" I felt down in my heart, broken and without hope.

Even though there were people around me, I had no real connections with anyone and my English was poor. No one reached out to me or told me about God. I thought if people knew I was from Iran they would hate me, so if they asked, I would tell them I was Persian, which is true. If they wanted to know where that was, I would simply tell them it was close to Russia.

I kept reading my Farsi Bible which made me feel a bit uncomfortable at times because it said that Jesus was the son of God. I had a problem with that: God didn't have a son, or so I thought. I knew Jesus was a prophet and He'd helped me; I decided to keep reading because of that. I was staying at my aunt and uncle's house and the second night in a row that I read the Bible it began to make me angry. On the third night, I read from the book of John (Johanna): "In the beginning was the Word and the Word was with God, and the Word was God. He was with God in the beginning. Through Him all things were made..." This made me so angry that I threw the Bible to the opposite corner of the room. "Jesus, thank you so much for helping me but this book is corrupted; not only do Christians claim Jesus is the son of God, but they claim Jesus is God Himself. I can't do this, this is blasphemy."

I had been in the States for three years, my English was improving and I decided to do some modelling. My hair was longer, I was young, and I started attending modelling and acting school. My acting teacher, Miss Dorsie, knew Jesus. She was non-religious and full of love. She reached out to me and when she spoke, she looked me in the eyes. I trusted her because she was genuinely interested in what was going on in my heart.

I told her about my life and my God. She asked me to share about the relationship I had with my God. I started to talk with passion because I always loved God, but I had to say, "I don't have any relationship with him." She remarked that I seemed angry with my God and I agreed that I was. I told her that I always wanted to be a friend of God but God didn't want to have a friend. She began to tell me about her God; about Jesus and the blood of Jesus. As a Muslim, blood makes you unclean. "Can blood wash your sin?" I wondered. Miss Dorsie spoke in a loving way and was genuinely interested in me, not trying to turn me into a Christian. One day she invited me to her birthday party. I trusted her and felt safe for the first time since I'd arrived in America.

It was there that I met some of her friends. One of them talked about Jesus with a passion. I was surprised when her friends really seemed to care about me. One thing intimidated me though; they were all smiling. I had never truly been happy nor smiled in my heart, so I thought perhaps it was because they were all living the 'American dream' and had plenty of money. I got to know them over time and came to realize this wasn't the reason they were smiling so much. We all became friends, but I didn't agree with everything they said such as 'God is love'; I didn't believe that.

I was thirty-three years old, and after all those years of seeking God fruitlessly I was sick and tired of talking about God. "If God is love," I thought, "He would connect me with His heart." I was at the end of myself and without hope. However, I had seen Jesus three years previously in my hotel room in Cyprus and He had helped me to get a visa. I began to wonder if I should give Him a chance, just this once, and see what would happen.

My new friends continued to be patient with me and I asked them: "How can I pray to this Jesus?" One of them told me the 'salvation' prayer but I didn't want to give my heart to Him; I wanted to pray in my own language and in my own way.

I began praying in Farsi and I said, *"Jesus, I don't believe you are the son of God, but if you are, I give you my heart. Jesus, I don't believe your blood has any power to forgive my sin, but if there is any forgiveness through your blood, please go ahead and wash all my sins away, I receive your blood. Jesus, if you can build a relationship with me in my heart and the heart of God, who you claim is your Father, I give you full permission to do anything you want to do with my heart, my life, with everything. You have complete and full permission. Do anything that you want to do."*

When I finished praying, I felt something physically touch me and I began to weep. It was such a moment of relief for me. Still I didn't believe that Jesus was who He said, but it was an amazing feeling; it felt so good, so cleansing. I'd never experienced that feeling before in my whole life.

Like something from an Indiana Jones movie, one thing in my life led to another and then another: a war-torn country, hunger for God, the Muslim God not responding, the love of people I met and suddenly a door was open. A huge lock seemed to open, and a heavy chain fell. I realized I had not been ready before that day, but on January 21st, 2000, I got saved. I prayed that prayer and even though I didn't believe that Jesus was the son of God I had opened my heart to Him. It was the first step and a massive leap for me. I discovered that Jesus listens as soon as we pray to Him, no matter what religion we are, or what path we have walked upon.

I felt safe enough when I got invited by Miss Dorsie and her friends to their church in Atlanta. But when I arrived and saw the thousands of people in attendance, I sat on the back row by myself. It was there that I was overwhelmed by a feeling of peace. I had never experienced peace like that. A tear rolled down my cheek. I was sitting there with my baggage. I was living in a country where people are afraid of Muslims, yet in this place I felt love and I felt peace. I couldn't understand why I was crying. "Perhaps this place reminds me of the Mosque?" I questioned. I didn't really understand what the

Pastor was saying but I felt comfortable and safe. I liked it.

I was invited a second time and sat in the same place. I felt the same peace, and a tear rolled down the same cheek. The third time I was invited, I was keen to go and drove there myself but I got lost on the way and was twenty minutes late. An usher led me to the very front row of the church. I was this tall Iranian Muslim guy, surrounded by American Christians and I felt conspicuous on the front row of that massive church. I didn't know what to do or how to behave. The Pastor began to preach and was walking across the large stage. Suddenly, the atmosphere changed. I could actually feel and see the atmosphere, it was really weird. I recognized the feeling; it was similar to when I first read the Bible in Cyprus. I looked at the Pastor and he appeared to be full of fire walking across the stage. Then, while he was walking, I saw another man standing behind him with a rod in his right hand. The atmosphere was so thick I could almost touch it.

The man with the rod looked at me. I was thinking, "Who is that?" and a voice inside me said it's Īsā Masīh, the Farsi name for Jesus Christ. A different voice demanded: "That's not Jesus. You just see stuff." I began to agree with the second voice. Just then, the man with the rod walked on air towards me and came down to the ground right in front of me. He then proceeded to walk into my body! It was like I was a door and He just walked in. Later I realized that I'd already opened the door when I prayed to Him. And now He was walking right into my heart. I saw His hand touch my heart and I felt fire throughout my body.

My heart was filled with fire and the peace I'd initially felt, seemed to multiply a thousand times. I was embraced by the Prince of Peace. My eyes were closed but I could see fire all around me and something like a milky fire consuming me; the most delicious fire ever. It felt so good. It felt like a hug from God, a hug of the Holy Spirit. He embraced me and received me: "It doesn't matter what you did, what you are doing, what you will do or not do, I am receiving all of you, no matter what."

I was crying, I was shaking, my nose was running, and I was embarrassed because God had embraced me in front of all those people. It was a bit like your parent kissing you all over your face when they're dropping you off at school. I was crying so hard and didn't want people to see me cry. I asked Him to stop and come back later!

I saw my friends at the end of the service and asked them what the fire and milky spirit was. They told me it was the Holy Spirit. I hadn't heard of Holy Spirit so I asked them what it was. "The Spirit of God" they told me. I was taken aback when they told me the Spirit of God came inside my body. I was about to answer that couldn't be what happened, but my whole body stopped me from saying it. "You're right," I answered, "The Spirit of God came into my body."

I savored the feeling; beautiful and delicious, God's love wrapped around me. All those years wanting to become a friend of God, yet never imagining an embrace by God like this, that it would be this good. That embrace turned my life upside down. Jesus became my life. I totally changed and everything after that was different; my view of life, the way I talked, the way I cried, the way I laughed, the way I looked at the sky, looked at the rain - it was literally like being born again. I had a completely new set of lenses.

Yet I still didn't believe Jesus was the son of God. I believed He was alive and had power to forgive my sin. "If He's the son of God, then He has to show me Himself" I surmised. My friends told me about another church in Georgia where apparently God spoke to people and showed them things about others. I was amazed that God would actually talk to a human being. I said, "Take me to that place!" But as soon as I arrived, I took offence. People were playing guitars and jumping up and down and I thought they looked very silly. However, I trusted my friends and what had happened to me, even though it seemed more like a nightclub than a church.

Some people started waving flags and I thought, "Oh God, what am I doing here?" I went over to the corner of the building, like I was standing by the wailing wall or something. I said, "Jesus, I don't know what these people are doing but I came here to see You." I took my seat, and despite being offended by those people worshipping God so exuberantly, I sensed something good was about to happen.

It was a Friday night and was a long service, with worship and then teaching. I wanted them to hurry up and get to the good stuff I'd gone there for. I was hoping someone would pray for me. Towards the end of the meeting when it was getting late, a group started walking down various aisles of the church. They would point people out and say, "I feel in my heart that God wants to tell you this…"

I was the eighth person they came to. I could feel my whole body shaking as they walked towards me. A lady who was probably 5'2" looked up to my 6'7" frame standing there and asked me my name. She asked if she could touch my hand, and as soon as she did, something inside of me reacted to something inside of her. I knew that whatever was residing inside of me was terrified of looking into her eyes. I turned my head sideways and shielded my eyes with my hand. "I tell that accusing spirit to let go of this man right now" she commanded. My English was not good, and I didn't know what an accusing spirit was. But whatever she said made me lose all my energy and I collapsed painlessly onto the floor. My eyes were closed, but with the eyes of my heart I saw a dark tornado forming in my stomach. It felt uncomfortable as the dark tornado moved up to my throat. I began to scream and yell. There were other forces living inside my body that I hadn't known about. The Bible calls it deliverance from evil spirits, but I had no idea at the time what was happening. Thankfully, they left and never came back.

Up until that moment, I strongly believed in the God and the prophet of Islam. They had been the support of my life, my identity. The foundation I had been standing on collapsed and my body collapsed at the same time. My eyes were closed but I could see far up into the sky, to heaven and I saw Jesus standing at the right side of a throne. The moment I saw Him, this milky thick Spirit came from heaven towards me, like a ray of light radiating from the sun. It touched my body and unlocked my very being. When the light touched my stomach, feelings of an atomic bomb of love exploded inside me.

I knew in that moment that for those twenty-one years of wanting to be a friend of God, Jesus, the son of God, was the one I had been searching for. All those years watching the door of my father's grocery store, it was Jesus I was waiting for. Every single moment I'd ever had, even eating food I loved, all those things came together and my whole body was saying, "Jesus - it was you all along."

Now looking back, I know it was the Father of our Lord Jesus Christ and the creator of heaven and earth, the only God of the universe, the only God who loves, who was calling me at that early age. He used everything around me to get my attention, whether a dream, a book, a friend, my mother's advice; God used it all.

I felt like an orphan whose father and mother are king and queen, but the orphan doesn't know its parents. One day the King will show up and say, "You are my son, you are my daughter, come to me." And that's what He did for me. I thought I had waited so long, but you know, God had waited much longer to meet me, and to meet you. He waits for you to meet your Father, your Maker, your Life. I was looking for the path, the way to walk on. I discovered the way is a person, He is Jesus. Now I have a relationship with Him. My country is not Iran or the United States; my country is Jesus Christ. I know that now.

After that experience, many great things happened. I started to pray for all my family members back home in Iran. One by one they had experiences with Jesus, and now my wife and I have several satellite programs that broadcast in Iran and millions of people are being touched, all over the Middle East.

Allow the Lord to touch your heart and your personality that you may love Him and know His love and love one another. If you've never been embraced by God, how can you embrace yourself or other people? I pray right now, if you want to have an experience with God, I ask for the Lord to embrace you in the way He embraced me. Any time you want to be embraced, just ask Him. He loves you.

Pray with Aliss:

"Father God, thank you that I can be your friend through your precious Son Jesus Christ. Set me free from anything that hinders that relationship so that I can know you fully and experience how wide and high and deep your love for me is, Amen."

Unexpected Miracles

Chapter Eight
LISA
Introducing Lisa

I met Lisa at one of our 'Supernatural' workshops in Chester. She and her Philippine husband were sitting on the front row. We often begin each workshop asking people to introduce themselves. When it was Lisa and her husband's turn, they briefly shared how they had been 'on the dark side' until recently and now wanted to learn how to operate in the supernatural through Jesus.

Subsequently, I got to know Lisa more and she shared with me her remarkable story. I was thrilled to discover that the shop we used to run in Chester, 'Spirit', had played a significant role in her dramatic encounter with the Living God.

LISA'S STORY

It started when I was just seven years old. My best friend believed in unicorns and magicians. One day I said, "I really like your hair bobble" and she quite matter-of-factly replied that it came from a magician. She shared with me a sort of magical prayer which would make a hair bobble manifest from the magician. I went outside into the garden and put my hands out really expecting with all my faith for a hair bobble to materialize and it did, the following day. I got the hair bobbles I wanted, but I also unconsciously opened a door in my life to the occult, even as a seven-year-old.

When I was eleven, my great aunt was suffering from grief having lost her sister (my grandmother), and she persuaded me to do the Ouija board with her. She wanted to communicate with my Grandma. Being young and naïve, I agreed. The door to the occult was opened even wider in my life. Half way through doing the Ouija board, my great aunt left the room briefly and whilst she was out, a photograph of my Grandma fell face down. I wondered if something or somebody was warning me not to continue.

I experienced a lot of supernatural things happening and I would see spirits and hear things that weren't physically there. I assumed this was quite normal. They didn't appear to be evil spirits at the time, but I saw illuminated faces appearing on the walls and moving around and spirits would speak to me during the night.

When I was sixteen my parents divorced and during that traumatic time, the spiritual phenomena escalated. That year after finishing school, I decided to study Beauty and Holistic Therapies. In addition to attending College, I worked in a salon and I would begin to know which clients were calling before I even answered the phone or before they walked into the salon. It was happening every day. Because of this, my Manager suggested I study Reiki, a type of spiritual healing.

I visited a Spiritualist Church and there was a Medium who showed us around. When he described the spirits he could see, I could already see them. Then as he performed mediumship on the stage, I would see spirits and other stuff moving around. I would have pursued the mediumship path headlong, but something seemed to prevent me from doing it and I just knew something in my heart told me not to. I realized later it was the Holy Spirit!

However, I decided to pursue my career in Reiki and other therapies. I was taught that Reiki originates from Buddhist roots, mixed up with Christianity. In Reiki when you place your hands onto people, you are taught to channel the universal energy flowing through you into others who need healing.

I completed Reiki level one training and when I became 'attuned' to the next level of Reiki, I felt pushed out of the picture as I literally saw spirits coming around the bed of the person that was receiving the 'healing.' I watched as they did the work so I was actually just facilitating a 'healing' space. But it was demons that were coming. They didn't look like demons at the time: they looked like heavenly beings, angels of light. Sometimes they seemed intergalactic. There's a lot of emphasis on the lost world of Atlantis in the New Age so sometimes they'd look like Atlantean guides and they took on many different forms. The person would be lying face down and receiving from demonic beings as I stood there watching and instructing what was going on.

A lot of Reiki practitioners are taught to protect themselves prior to conducting the healing session but in reality that can never really happen because you can't protect yourself from a demonic spirit that you have invited in. Inevitably you're sacrificing your own health – spiritually, physically and mentally, to facilitate the 'healing' of the other person. I was always physically tired from doing the Reiki but I just had a big heart for people and wanted to see them get well.

I then became involved with crystals. I would douse over the energy centers using a pendulum to check the chakras. Much of the teaching of the chakras is based on the Kabbalistic tree of life which is counterfeit, as the true tree of life is Jesus, but I didn't know that at the time. There is some power in the counterfeit, but it is limited and doesn't bring wholeness. I felt as though I was on a roller coaster; high during a Reiki or Pranic session and then low, just like with any drug.

Originally, I practiced Reiki from home and then I went out to Dubai to work at a Spa with connections to Egyptian mysticism. I was very connected with the all-seeing eye of Horus, often used in the occult. I met a woman there who said, "I've been waiting four years for you to get here to do Pranic healing with me." We were working with chakras more, energy systems of the body, both physically and spiritually. We thought we were casting out demonic spirits with the Pranic psychotherapy. It originates from Buddhism and is connected with Reiki. I was doing a lot of different courses such as Arhatic Yoga and I became a Pranic healing instructor as well, so I was teaching other people how to do it.

I also practiced reflexology. I was taught that reflexology works on energy pathways, energy lines which go up from each foot and then cross over and meet at 'chakras.' It is supposed to work on the different organs and tissues of the body which are mirrored in the feet so when you manipulate the feet it causes a healing response in the body.

Around this time I met and married my husband. He's from the Philippines and we met at a Pranic

Healing group. After a while, things in our marriage began to get difficult. Part of it was a clash of cultures, but also, as I began to discover, New Age practices often result in broken or unhealthy relationships. If I'm honest, our marriage was probably on the brink of divorce at this point.

One day I was just flicking through the TV channels when I came across a Christian channel that was showing a program called, 'Marriage Today'. We needed help in our marriage and the more I watched, the more answers I was getting. It was based on God's Kingdom principles and all seemed to make so much sense to me. I couldn't stop watching it. I ended up praying along with them, but I didn't realize at that time just how profound that prayer would be.

However, two months later I graduated as a Reiki Master. I worked hard and was building my beauty and holistic therapies business up. I had plenty of clients and was working in a warehouse with other salon services. One day I was chatting to another woman who worked there and she asked me what I did. I explained about the holistic therapies and Pranic healing and she told me she was a hairdresser. I don't know how we got talking about it, but I remember saying to her, "Well, all roads lead to Rome." She looked at me and replied, "No, actually they don't" and I felt this almighty conviction like someone had booted me in my stomach. I remember after she'd gone, saying to myself, "I feel really weird like something's just happened." From a New Age point of view, I thought she'd just stolen my energy or something, but that feeling wouldn't leave and I had this sense of guilt.

That wasn't the only experience I had. God was after me. Even though I couldn't ignore the signs, I continued on the New Age path, but time and time again, the Lord gently but firmly let me know that He was real and He had another way for me that was better.

The first time I went into Aliss' shop, 'Spirit', in Chester, I saw a beautiful French painted chair in the window. We were decorating our bedroom and I felt it would be perfect. Then I noticed a chalk board next to it which said, 'Free Healings and Miracles.' I thought, "What? Free healings and miracles!?", so I went straight in. I got chatting to the Manager, Margaret and asked what they did. She explained that they prayed for people. I thought, "Pray for people!? How can that work?" She came right out and asked me, "Do you know Jesus?" to which I replied, "Yeah, I know Jesus." I really thought I did know Him at the time, but I was deceived. I didn't know Him. She grabbed my hands and said, "Do you know how much Jesus loves you?" and I said, "Yeah," but I didn't. I felt a strong presence of God in that moment.

Soon afterwards, something dramatic happened. I was in the middle of a Reiki treatment and I was watching who I thought was 'Jesus' doing the healing, using universal energy. Suddenly, the real Jesus appeared in the treatment room. He said, "Stop this now!" The whole energy of the room completely shifted and there was this almighty power that came in like I'd never experienced before. True, perfect power and love. I didn't feel condemnation, but I knew it was the truth.

After that, I began to question what I was doing and one day I said, "Jesus, if you want me to follow you, give me a tangible sign." That same day, I was in Chester and had to walk past a man who was preaching about Jesus. I kept walking, trying to ignore him, but his eyes fixed on mine and he began to walk towards me and came straight up to me. I was a bit taken aback, especially with what happened next. He reached into his pocket and pulled out a laminated sign which he handed to me. I'd asked God that day for a tangible sign from Him and here was a guy I didn't know, preaching about Jesus and giving me a literal sign with John 3:16 written on it. I read the words, "For God so loved the world that He gave His only Son, so that whoever believes in Him should not perish but would have eternal life." What an amazing God! That was a sign I just couldn't ignore.

Over the following days I received other signs, such as leaflets I found stuffed inside pockets with words saying "Jesus gives you peace" - they all seemed to come out of nowhere! I bought a suit jacket for my husband and in the pocket was another leaflet on Jesus! Something similar happened on three different occasions.

I went back into Aliss' shop to buy a couple of books and got chatting with a volunteer who, I found out much later, was Aliss' mother, Hazel. This was before I made the decision to follow Jesus. Hazel asked me my name and she told me hers, just before I left the shop. Then as I continued down the street, who should come up to me but the street preacher again and he asked me my name. I told him it was Lisa and he said, "There are kind people with the name Lisa, a bit like Hazel" and off he walked, just like that.

God was melting my heart and drawing me to Him, bit by bit. He is so wonderful. I was really wanting to give my life to Him completely and follow Him, but one of the stumbling blocks for me was that my life was built around so many New Age practices. My career, my income, my friends, even my husband, who I'd met at a New Age group. My whole life had been built on counterfeit spirituality and I didn't know how to make the changes I knew I needed to.

I was on social media one day and noticed that a friend of mine, also a Reiki practitioner, had written a post on Facebook highlighting the benefits of Reiki. Underneath, someone had written quite a convicting message saying that she used to be into the occult, she knows that Reiki is not of God, and to turn her back on it. I can't remember the exact wording, but as soon as I read that, I couldn't stop crying. I remember saying to my mother, "What I'm doing is wrong and I just feel so bad and I feel like I've built a business based on this, how do I get rid of this? How do I get free from this?" My mum simply replied, "Just don't do it anymore!" I felt I was so wrapped up in it that I didn't know how to get free. But somehow, God gave me the courage I needed to break free and to stop putting my trust in Reiki and in my business and truthfully, it's the best thing I've ever done.

I realized later through practicing all these counterfeit healing methods that you can never heal yourself, it's only through the power of Jesus the Son of God that you can be whole. I've come across quite a few Christians who have got involved with some of these New Age healing methods, either practicing them or going for treatments. They don't seem to realize where the root of it lies and how dangerous it is. Anything that gets its source of power outside of Jesus is a counterfeit and that's the reality of it. I used to feel empowered by people coming to see me for treatments but that is wrong as I was exalting myself above Jesus and that's not good.

We are given the tool of prayer to release strongholds, to heal others and that's what we're commissioned to do as Christians, so why mix the counterfeit with the truth? I always wanted to glorify God, that was in my heart, but I went down the wrong path. As soon as I found out I was not doing God's work and I was not glorifying God, I stopped. And that's when He saved me.

It's amazing how Jesus will show you how intimately He knows you. I was stunned by all the ways God proved His love to me and delivered me powerfully from all that had entangled me. I had been ensnared by the enemy from a young age and now I was about to get free. I finally made that choice to give my life fully to Jesus and I decided to give up all the New Age practices and counterfeit spirituality and power. I renounced all that was not from God and I asked Jesus to come into my life and set me free from all the past. I was born again: a new creation!

When it came to my business, I had many clients; I had my own shop as well as other practitioners working with me. They were doing Reiki and crystal therapy and at first I tried to subcontract the work to them but I felt like I was cheating God, so I just got rid of it. Everything. It was difficult because after building up the business and growing my list of clients and getting to know them, I gave my life to Jesus. It wasn't something I initially shared with other people so it was awkward trying to explain to people why I was closing the business. I felt like I was at a crossroads. I knew God was calling me to some sort of ministry and I kept shaking it off and then it all came to a head and I thought, "Okay God, if you want me to surrender my life completely to you, you're gonna have to help me close the shop."

God began to show me little by little how He was going to help me make the transition. I'd gone from New Age to Christian and was a new person, but my surroundings were still the same. I decided to join a local church and it was there that God gave me a clear message: Replace the buddhas. So that day I went and bought some wall art fish and a tree and I got rid of the buddhas in the shop. I had a vision during the worship time in church where I saw Jesus glorified on top of the shop. Then I clearly saw the shop crumbling quickly to the ground and the Lord said, "I'm going to destroy and rebuild this temple in three days." So I knew that was it – done. And that's what happened. It closed that quickly in a matter of days, just like He'd shown me. My whole life has changed and I'm now doing a degree in Theology and Evangelism. I'm excited to see what God's got in store for me next.

God has transformed my marriage. He healed it, he healed our marriage and helped me realize that a lot of the problems were me! God works on your character before he works on anything else. When I first became a Christian, my husband opposed it a little because he was also fully into New Age practices like I had been. He couldn't really understand how I could have gone from all of that to suddenly being a Christian. But as God's been doing more and more work in me, my husband has seen the changes and started to come to church. Then recently he received Jesus into his life properly. He now has a relationship with Jesus and has seen really positive changes. He's reading the Bible and he wants to work for God as well in ministry. That's why we both went to the Supernatural Workshop that Rob and Aliss did.

At the workshop, my husband was delivered from a spirit of anger. He'd been holding onto it since his parents both sadly died within a short space of time, plus a lot of other trauma he went through early in our marriage. One of the other workshop attendees was given a word of knowledge by the Holy Spirit about my husband who was so amazed that God loved him that much that He had given such specific information to a complete stranger. The guy had dealt with something similar in his life some years before and was literally in the middle of writing a chapter about it in a book that morning! He prayed with my husband who was set completely free. We're both wanting to fully give our lives to Jesus and follow Him and help other people do the same.

One of the chilling things I learned is that I thought I was following God all those years and helping people by the New Age therapies, but I discovered it was a complete deception by the enemy. The enemy subtly takes some of the counterfeit teachings that I was involved in, and mixes them with Biblical principles, but distorting them.

It was a huge turning point for me when the real Jesus walked into my treatment room as I thought I was watching 'Jesus' doing Reiki. I was operating in a degree of spiritual power which I thought was from God, but when I encountered the true and ultimate power of Jesus, I realized I had been plugging into the wrong socket! The power of the Holy Spirit does the work, I didn't need to have anything else channelling through me. Jesus is the healer. But I had to submit my life to Him and be full of His Holy Spirit for His power to flow through me.

Why would you want to mix the counterfeit with the truth? Why settle for much less than the real deal, the highest power in the Universe who is Jesus, the Son of God? As soon as I found out I was not doing God's work and glorifying Him, I stopped the Reiki and Pranic healing and all the other New Age practices. Now I have given my life to Jesus, I am experiencing so much more power which is pure and an increased love for others.

I needed to go through a time of recovery because I had based my life on a lie; the devil had stolen my identity and I based my own value on my career. What helped me enormously was reading the book of Ephesians in the Bible. I discovered the truth of my identity as God's precious child and I pray that you also discover through Jesus just how precious you are to Him and your true identity as a chosen child of God.

Pray with Aliss:

"Lord, I ask that you remove any veil from my mind and my heart that is preventing me from knowing the truth about who you are and how precious I am to you. Help me discover the depths of love you have for me. If I am not walking in the good path that you have destined for my life, or if I am basing my worth and my identity on anything but you, please show me and help me to make the changes, Amen."

Chapter Nine
MATT
Introducing Matt

I awoke in the middle of the night with a strong feeling that I should get up and out of bed. I had an overwhelming urge to pray! Often the Holy Spirit wakes me up in the night to pray, but usually I stay in bed and can pray there for hours under my warm duvet. But this particular night, I felt I was to go into my study and get on my knees. I was there for a few hours praying. I didn't know exactly who I was praying for, but I knew it was for more than one person who was about to get right with God and start a new life with Him. I kept praying for them that night until the 'urge to pray' had lifted, which it did a few hours later. I remember praying that I would meet them that day, whoever they were, and that an angel would pull them into our café. I prayed for them to be hungry for God, not just a cooked breakfast!

Later that day something amazing happened. I was working in the café when two long haired, tattooed guys in their twenties came in: Matt and Mark. They were the guys I'd been praying for all night. I'll let Matt tell you the story.

MATT'S STORY

I'm really into rock music. Me and my best friend Mark have always been huge fans of the American rock band 'Korn'. One day we heard that Korn's lead guitarist, Brian 'Head' Welch had left the band because he wanted to try and get his life straightened out. It was well known that he was addicted to drugs and alcohol. He was an absolute mess and he was probably close to death from either suicide or a drug overdose. He began to ask his friends for help and one of them suggested that he go to church. Brian is one of the biggest rock stars in the world and he was like, "Erm – I don't think so", but then eventually he went to church and he gave his life over to Jesus.

His life transformed dramatically as a result, along with his bass player Fieldy. I've still yet to meet him - one of these days, hopefully. 'Head' was mine and Mark's hero and I began to think that if 'Head' had changed by giving his life to Jesus, then maybe it would work for me too.

But I've always been a 'believe it when I see it' sort of person. So something dramatic needed to happen in my life to really make me want to take the plunge and give my life to Christ like 'Head' had. I was spending most of my time listening to music, I was in a band but not really doing much. I was drinking all the time: always, always drinking and drinking and it was like that was our thing, that was our way of partying and blocking out reality. It was just a dull existence really.

On this particular day, Mark came round to my house and he was like "Dude, I need to get this book." Mark was dyslexic you see, so I had to help him with reading, but he didn't tell me which book he wanted. It was funny because I also wanted a book that day; I'd woken up wanting to get a Bible, just to see what it was all about. But I was too embarrassed to tell Mark that I wanted a Bible. We left my house to go into Chester and we actually walked past Aliss' café to catch the bus, but we just thought it was an empty building with metal grilles at the window, we had no idea it was a café.

We got on a bus and walked around the city all day looking for our books. Neither of us had mentioned to the other which book we wanted until Mark finally admitted, "I'm actually looking for a Bible." We couldn't believe it when we realized we both wanted to buy a Bible. So we walked to a Christian bookshop, found some Bibles and paid for them. On the bus ride back home, we opened up the Bibles and tried to read them but we were like, "Ye olde thy thou what?" We had no idea what it meant but reckoned we'd figure it out when we got home.

As we passed Aliss' café again, Mark turned and said, "How long's this been here for, man?" Before we knew it, we were inside. We ordered coffees and, feeling a bit bewildered, we remarked that we'd not seen the place before. Aliss told us that it was a 'Jesus' café. Our jaws almost hit the floor, you know, like in a cartoon. It was crazy. Aliss began to tell us about Jesus and we told her about the Bibles and how we were surprised to end up in the café and how it felt as though something had pulled us in.

Aliss explained that the Holy Spirit had woken her up and had her praying for us all night, even though she'd never met us and didn't know who she was praying for. But she knew some people were going to encounter Jesus that day and she'd asked for the angels standing outside the café to pull the right people in.

We could hardly believe it! We showed Rob and Aliss our Bibles and they smiled when we told them we couldn't understand the old English versions. They then replaced them with newer translations and everything sort of fell into place.

It really felt like somebody was watching over us - it was very weird, like an angel *had* pulled us in. Whilst Aliss was talking about Jesus, I knew it was who I wanted to meet. I mentioned in passing that I had a problem with my knee and she said Jesus could heal people and do miracles. In my head I was like, "Nah" but I let her pray for my knee and then I said, "OK, this really is weird." She didn't actually place her hand on my knee but held it just over the top and I felt this really warm energy going through my knee and I felt my knee going right. It was then that I knew this was totally real. (And I've had no more problems with my knee at all since then).

Rob and Aliss told us some more about Jesus and then gave me a booklet with a daily reading from the Bible and some notes which explained it. The next morning, the sun was shining and I was smiling because of how mental it all was. Mark and I walked down the road with my dog and I turned to the page in the booklet with the scripture for the day and it stopped me in my tracks. I read the first line and Mark was like, "What's the matter dude?" I read it out loud: "Imagine walking down a path, walking your dog with the sun shining." It was unbelievable. We knew God was talking to us and He had our attention.

That evening Rob and Aliss were holding a 'School of the Spirit' meeting and me and Mark went along to it. We hadn't actually given our lives to Jesus at that point; we were just getting freaked out by it all. Aliss invited us up to the front of the meeting to share what had been happening to us those two days. There were a lot of people in there, all focused on us while we were talking and they seemed just as gob-smacked as we were when they heard the whole story. Aliss asked if we had given our lives to Jesus yet and put the microphone close to me. I was just like "No" and laughing as I didn't know what to say. I felt a bit intimidated and was just trying to block out the people watching.

The next day I was sitting on my bed and I'd just finished playing my guitar when I decided to pick up another booklet that Aliss had given me. In the back was a prayer with the words, "If you say this prayer, you're accepting Jesus into your life" and I thought, "You know what? I'm gonna do it." I read it and I remember saying, "…in Jesus' name, Amen." Suddenly, I felt like someone had their arms around me giving me a big hug. It felt good.

Mark gave his life to Jesus too, and soon afterwards Rob and Aliss baptized us in a kiddie's paddling pool in their back garden. It was Easter weekend and the forecast was for torrential rain all day and cold weather. We were all in the kitchen, reluctant to go out, but Aliss went outside, pointed to the black clouds and told them to leave and for the sun to come out. Seconds later the sun was shining and we were able to go outside into the warm sunny garden! We were relieved and so were all the other people there to celebrate the baptism with us. People were checking their phones and the forecast was still terrible.

Unfortunately, the kiddie pool was so small we had to kneel, and the water was freezing. Despite the sunshine, I'm sure my lips were turning blue. But it was an amazing experience as I gave my life fully to Jesus with all our church family cheering us on.

I remember one time we went to a church in Wales with Aliss. She was speaking about Jesus and then she invited me and Mark up to the front to speak to everyone too. I looked at Mark and we were like, "What do we say!?" We decided we'd go with whatever came to mind. We jumped up to the front and told them some of our story. We helped Aliss to pray for people and release miracles and then I said, "If anybody wants to talk about anything just feel free to come over." Near enough the entire room was surrounding us and we had no idea what to do as we were fresh new Christians. Mark and I had always made a good team when it came to giving people advice and stuff, so we took it all in our stride and tried to rely on the Holy Spirit's wisdom as we helped encourage people and prayed with them.

Initially things went from strength to strength spiritually, but my fiancée and I broke up, Mark moved away and then I moved away too and lost contact with Rob and Aliss and my church family for a few years. Things started to take a downward spiral. I tried to make things better for myself and believed I was a good person but I wasn't really following Jesus fully and gradually everything started to crush me mentally. Things were getting to me and over time I realized that I was suffering from depression. It was so, so hard. I would often wake up in the morning and sit on the edge of my bed and in my thoughts I would hear, "You're not going to be here anymore, you don't deserve to be here anymore." It was the hardest thing I've ever had to deal with in my life. I realized later that it was an evil spirit speaking these things, but at the time I thought it was me and I didn't know what to do.

I recognized that I needed help and had to do something. I remember saying to someone later that if I had a gun at that time, I probably would have shot myself. But the depression went on for four years and I didn't tell anybody for all that time and that's probably the worst thing I ever did. I was in another relationship by that point, and I couldn't even tell my girlfriend how I was feeling because I didn't want to upset her. I was just closed off from everyone. I was working as a garbage collector at that time, but I didn't enjoy the job. So I left and took a job in sales at a builders' store, something I had no experience of but I decided to try something new in an effort to get out of depression.

It was good initially and I was excited thinking, "This is it, this is a step in a new direction." But because I was inexperienced and was offered no training, I would do things wrong and I realized my job wasn't the answer. I wasn't hitting my sales targets and began to sink lower and lower into depression. I knew I needed to get out of there but one day a member of staff asked me why I was looking so sad. Reluctantly, I admitted to him that I was suffering from depression. I'd finally told somebody and he encouraged me by saying, "We'll work together on this, we'll help you through it." I breathed a sigh of relief as I'd finally plucked up enough courage to tell someone and he seemed to not only understand, but to want to help me overcome it. Then I told another Manager how hard it was to take on this new job and suffer with depression at the same time. He told me that if I needed to vent my feelings, I could go up to the top of the store and clear my head. He said, "We'll work together on this." That evening back home I felt positive for the first time in a long while.

However, the very next day when I went back into work, I was told I no longer had a job. I was dumbfounded. Surely things could not get any worse. I felt my life was over. I felt like I had let everyone down. I'd had enough. I knew I'd got to go. I had to end it. I left my house and walked away. I walked and kept walking for miles. I didn't care where I was going. I found myself on a bridge beside the River Dee with a train track behind me. I stopped and thought, "What a perfect place to go. This is it; game over."

There was a railing which ran along the edge of the bridge, so I grabbed it and pulled myself up. I managed to get my foot onto the railing and knew that in a few seconds it would all be over. It was one of the most surreal moments of my life and it's hard to fully explain, but as I pushed myself up into the air, up into my final breaths, unseen arms grabbed me and pulled me back to the ground. I spun around angrily swinging my right fist at whoever was pulling me back from my ending but as I turned there was not a soul to be seen.

I looked up to the sky and shouted, "What are you doing!?" I didn't believe it. I didn't care. I picked myself up and began to walk again. I kept walking and eventually sat down, exhausted. I cried out, "If anyone can hear me now please take me away. I'm not going to fight you. You can mug me, beat me up and kill me. I don't care." And I shut my eyes wanting it to be for the last time. All at once a fresh breeze swept across my face, like when my grandmother would give me a playful slap. It was God's wake up call. I chose to pick myself up. I looked up to the sky and smiled. "OK God, I surrender." Everything began to fall into place after that.

One night I had a dream that my grandad visited me. Everything was bright white and my grandad came and sat next to me on a brick wall. He looked at me and shook his head. "What?" I asked. He told me, "I'm proud of you mate. No matter what, we're all proud of you" and then I woke up. I knew that Jesus had orchestrated that dream and that I'd seen my grandad in heaven. I had such a strong feeling when I woke up that I wanted to be back with my family in heaven, it was crazy, but I knew that it wasn't my time yet.

I hadn't seen my dad in a while, but I decided to go and tell my dad about the dream. He confirmed that he was proud of me and that not a day goes by when he's not proud of me. That rocked my world.

Soon afterwards I got back in contact with an old friend who's now the rhythm guitarist in my band and it turned out to be a God thing. He was there at just the right moment. He is so full of the Holy Spirit - I've seen people high on drugs but this is something else; he's high on the Most High! He's a great guy and I've got a lot to thank him for because he has helped me through.

I retrained in security and got myself a good job in my new career. I then got back in touch with Rob and Aliss almost accidentally. I was on social media listening to a song by a Christian rock band called Disciple. The track was titled 'The right time' and as I was singing along to the lyrics, "You came just at the right time," Rob's name popped up on Facebook and I thought, "It's a sign!" I got back in contact with Rob and now here I am telling him and Aliss all about my life since I last saw them.

If you are feeling down or suffering from depression or feel you can no longer carry on, please go and speak to somebody. Whether it's a friend, someone in your family, in a church nearby, a doctor or a support group. If you keep it to yourself and bottle it inside, then it won't end well for you or for those around you. Be honest and brave and open up to someone you can trust. Ask Jesus to come into your life. Life has its ups and downs but He's always there, He's always constant. Like I said earlier, I'm a person that believes when I see it and I saw it.

I love the way that to know God you just need to receive His love and to love Him back. He's great! I talk to God but I don't tend to ask Him for everything I need. I do my bit and I work hard and I thank Him for the good things He blesses me with. God shows me what I need to do, I put my mind to it and work at it, and He's there overseeing it all. I pray that you will know Him and His good plans for your life.

Pray with Aliss:

"Lord God help me to be honest with myself, with others, and with you. Help me to admit that I need others to help me. I'm sorry for any pride in my life and for thinking that I can do it all without you or without others around me. I thank you Father God that I am not alone or rejected; you have adopted me into your family and I am your valued and accepted child. You have a plan and a purpose for my life that is far better than I could know. I choose to surrender my life to you from this day forward, Amen."

Unexpected Miracles

Chapter Ten
ALEX

Introducing Alex

I first met Alex when he came to the boutique B&B we used to run, Little Mollington Hall, on his honeymoon. His Colombian wife had booked them both onto a 'Spiritual Retreat' that we were hosting in Chester.

He didn't know what he was coming to, but he trusted his new wife and hoped that, since he participated in a 'New Age' group, the 'Spiritual Retreat' would benefit him. I'll let him share his story in his own words.

ALEX'S STORY

I'm from Germany and for my whole life I've been on a journey. I was always searching for something more. As a teenager, I was interested in what my martial arts teacher had to say because I knew there was more attached to it than just sport. I was always searching for more, but never really knew what it was that I was looking for.

I spent eighteen months in China and then moved back to Germany where I became involved in running a successful business, supplying holistic frequency machines, as the CEO. I travelled to other countries with my work, setting up new markets and expanding the company. Despite all this, there was no real joy in my life. I was a bit of a loner and a deep thinker. I would spend a lot of time thinking things through and trying to gain understanding.

I knew there was more to life and was searching for something else; a deeper meaning, something spiritual. It was then that I got involved with a group of like-minded people who were also on a spiritual journey and wanted to experience more. I guess you could say that we were 'New Age.' We would meet together on a regular basis and explore meditation and other things.

I love languages and decided to study for a Degree in Chinese. I studied Chinese Business and Intercultural Communication. One evening there was a 'Chinese party' in my home city of Munich as part of the course. I didn't really want to go, but as it was part of my degree course, I felt obliged to. It was there that I met Margaret. She is Colombian but had been living in Germany for nine years and she was also studying for a degree in Chinese. She's a clever lady who speaks Spanish, Italian, German, Chinese and English. It turned out she didn't want to go to the party either, but we were attracted to each other and I loved the joy in her life. Our relationship blossomed and eventually we got engaged.

Margaret had been brought up as a Christian and talked to me about Jesus, but I wasn't really interested and was happy attending my 'New Age' spiritual group. I say happy, but really I had no joy in my life. One thing that attracted me to Margaret was her joy. She showed me what real joy was. It was difficult for us to be in a relationship as she was a Christian and I was not. I wanted her to move to my way of thinking a bit more, and she wanted me to know Jesus and so there was always this tension.

A couple of months before we got married, we felt like something needed to change. We knew things weren't right in our lives and I thought maybe we should go to China and start a new business or get involved in more studies. Margaret kept telling me to wait. She said, "Wait until the end of September; there will be something happening in September." I was skeptical but she was adamant that something good was going to happen then. She didn't know for sure, but she just had that sense and wasn't budging even when I tried to talk her out of it.

As soon as we were married, everything changed for me. As part of our honeymoon in September, Margaret had arranged flights to the UK and told me she'd booked us onto a 'Spiritual Retreat' at a place called 'Little Mollington Hall' in Chester. She'd discovered Aliss through seeing her on the TV and she wanted to go and meet her. When she'd been excited about something happening in September, she had no idea that she was receiving a prophetic prompting about the Retreat. As soon as Margaret saw the details, she took the opportunity of our honeymoon to book us onto it.

Margaret knew that there was something missing in my life and hoped that a trip to Chester would help me. I hadn't realized initially that it was a Christian Retreat. But I thought perhaps if I went with her to this, she would come round to my way of thinking. I was intrigued by the Spiritual Retreat and didn't know what to expect but I was keen to have new spiritual experiences. I had no idea that it was about to change my life.

What was strange was that there seemed to be so many 'coincidences' happening, more than I'd ever experienced before. For example, the Retreat was supposed to have eight participants but became four at the last minute, which was perfect for us. It was a very private kind of Retreat and it was led by Rod and Michelle who were working with Rob and Aliss. At that point in my spiritual journey, they were the perfect teachers for me. They weren't 'religious' like I was expecting when I eventually discovered it was a Christian Retreat.

I arrived at the Retreat with leg problems and internal abdominal issues. I'm not a depressive kind of person but I had become withdrawn and insular and kept other people at arm's length, so no-one else could really reach me. I learned to function like that for some time, but I knew there was something not right. One evening on the Retreat we had a 'soaking' session. Michelle and Rod prayed for me and I could really feel an energy circling inside my body and a heaviness and burden on my body being lifted. This kind of session was new for me. We sat on the sofas and it was a wonderfully relaxing and peaceful atmosphere with Christian music playing.

In all my previous spiritual experiences, I had never encountered anything like this. Everything that happened during the soaking session; every inner vision, every feeling, every sense of something happening, was good. This was new for me because until that day I always had to do something externally to help relax my mind. But during that session I could just let go without even trying. I'd done meditation before, but nothing like this. I didn't need to be convinced that what I felt was real. It was a big deal to me. I was really moved by what happened during that session.

Of course, this all made me interested in knowing Jesus more, and who He is. I knew Christianity in theory, I'd been baptized when I was a little child as a Protestant, but I'd never heard about people wanting to follow Jesus and actually living like Christians. This whole thing just never occurred to me until I went to Little Mollington Hall. In that moment I was deeply touched personally. Also, all my leg pain vanished and soon after, my abdomen pain was gone.

Over that weekend I felt a very strong pull to give my life to Jesus. It's hard to describe but it felt the right thing, in fact the only possible thing to do. What's unusual was the fact that I generally think very deeply. Normally I would need to think long and hard about a major decision like that, but at that particular moment it was more my heart going for it and my mind trying to catch up. It was so liberating. I felt such a strong desire to give my life to Jesus, so I did. We prayed a prayer, then Rod and Michelle explained a little more about Jesus and what was happening as I prayed.

During that prayer they said my face changed color a couple of times and they could see that things were going on. I couldn't see myself from the outside of course, but when I gave my life to Jesus and I invited Him into my life, the overwhelming feeling for me was that I no longer felt alone. I have a wonderful wife and wonderful family so I wasn't alone in that sense, but previously I had felt the kind of loneliness that nothing can fill. I had a loneliness that no other being on this planet, no money, nothing could satisfy, but in that moment as I gave my life to Jesus, that sense of loneliness and emptiness vanished. It was like going from zero to a hundred in a second. And that feeling has continued. I no longer feel alone. I now have a strong presence of Jesus in my life and have done ever since I invited Him in. In fact, the longer I'm following Him, the stronger His presence gets.

Before I went to the Retreat, I didn't know what was going on inside of me. I didn't know I was so alone. Even people close to me would say they had a sense of something missing but they didn't know what it was. They would ask me if everything was alright with me. I've changed so much since then. I was used to that internal state - it was a normal feeling for me, but I always knew something was not quite right there, and that's what propelled me to keep searching.

Before we married, my wife would pray for me and have others pray. All these things were very important to lead me to that point where I could accept and receive the experience I had at the Retreat and allow me to open up and invite Jesus into my life.

Margaret and I knew we were supposed to be together but it was difficult having a Christian and a non-Christian together in a relationship, yet God made it work. I am so blessed that Margaret is rooted so deeply in Christ that there is no way, nothing on this planet that can take her from that.

After the weekend Retreat, everything changed for us. When we arrived back home, newly married and newly saved, we felt that we should give up our jobs. Both of us were working for the same company, me as the CEO and Margaret as the Marketing Manager. We were successful at what we did, but something didn't seem right somehow. We also felt a strong connection with Little Mollington Hall and the team there. Amazingly we were invited to go back there and start an internship in the new year. It was one of those decisions that was easy for us; we just knew we were supposed to go back. There was no fear, no worries - there was just peace, peace, peace on that decision. So the two of us gave up our careers, packed up all our belongings, left our apartment and arrived back in Chester for an adventure. I had just given my life to Jesus and there was so much I needed and wanted to learn.

We spent about eight months on the internship. We learned so much and experienced more than we could have done had we stayed in Germany in our jobs. During the time we were there, Rob and Aliss hosted two residential 'Supernatural Schools' at

Little Mollington Hall. We were living there, so we were part of the schools too. People came from many countries for the month-long schools to learn and be activated in the supernatural. The schools were very important to me. I just sucked up everything, all the teaching and the Bible studies and the practical activations; I was like a sponge.

During the second school, we were asked if we'd like to run groups in the evenings. It was a lot of fun to practically exercise what we were learning during the day with the whole group. There was this lovely lady from Canada called Bonnie and we were talking about how people can experience gold dust on their hands or face. Bonnie said she'd love for that to happen to her, as a sign of God's presence. Quietly I prayed that God would do it. All of a sudden while we were talking about it, Bonnie looked at her hands and they were covered in gold dust. To be honest, I couldn't believe it at first and I was scrubbing her hands thinking it was makeup or something. I could really sense the presence of the Holy Spirit at the same time. The more we looked at her hands, the more gold dust appeared. We took pictures and were showing the others and it was an experience that impacted all of us in that moment; a visual confirmation of God's glory and presence.

I decided I wanted to be baptized. Margaret said she'd join me. We thought it should be out in nature rather than a pool, as it felt more authentic. Some of the other students came too so we all went together to the River Dee in Chester. A couple of people told me beforehand how their baptism was an amazing experience and of course this created a certain kind of hope inside me that I would experience the same thing. I was a bit disappointed that as I went down into the water I didn't feel anything spiritual and it happened so fast. But afterwards, after we'd come up out of the water we stood together, we prayed and a couple of people had a prophetic word for Margaret and me. It was just so peaceful.

We went out for some food afterwards and as I talked to my wife, we felt such peace that I knew something was going on. During the next couple of days I could sense in the spirit realm that things were shifting. It was such a good feeling. Since finishing the internship in Chester, Margaret and I have moved to the West Coast of America where we are part of Bethel Church's Supernatural School in Redding, California. We are following Jesus with all our hearts and going from strength to strength, learning how to minister to other people too.

I want to encourage anyone reading this if, like me, you feel that there is more. That what you have in your life and what you've experienced up to this point can't be all there is. There definitely is so much more and it all lies in Jesus Christ, it all lies in God our creator. It's not like I understand it all - I want to understand more but what I do know is that giving my life to Jesus has had a huge impact. It changed basically everything more than I could imagine and I'm convinced that it'll do the same for you too. Jesus is the one you're searching for.

Pray with Aliss:

"Lord God, I know there is more available to me than what I have experienced so far. I ask that you increase my capacity and fill me with the knowledge of you with the wisdom that comes from the Holy Spirit. Come and fill every part of me; remove all the loneliness and feelings of frustration. Quiet my mind and help me encounter you in my spirit, soul and body, Amen."

Chapter Eleven
DEBRA
Introducing Debra

Debra came to one of our conferences in Chester. Her name wasn't Debra at the time, it was another name she'd given herself; an occult name. The first time I met her was as I called her out in the meeting and she came up onto the stage.

She bravely told me and the hundreds of people at the conference how her life had recently been impacted by God and the dramatic turnaround that had subsequently happened. I'll let her share her story with you.

DEBRA'S STORY

I became a 'White Witch' in the 1990s and was part of several covens. I was involved as a witch for a number of years and I was also drawn into Druidism, Hinduism, Buddhism, New Age and Theosophy, but my life always seemed to be a struggle. One awful day, my partner attacked me and a friend with a knife. It was such an horrific thing to happen to me that after the incident, I began to suffer from post-traumatic stress. Nothing I tried could help my state of mind. I went to see my doctor who prescribed anti-depressants, but these didn't help and made things worse; the medication seemed to just shut me down.

I felt completely powerless from the knife attack and wanted something in my life that would help empower me. I bought books on voodoo and began to cast spells using voodoo, then delved into black witchcraft and satanism. I ended up making a pact with the devil and as I did this, demons entered and began tormenting me. I was enticed into buying more and more books to study, but ironically, the more power I searched for, the less I was in control and the more the demons had power over me. I would hear voices in my head telling me what to do and I knew I was coming under a dark influence, but I didn't know how to stop.

As I continued in the occult, demons would speak loudly in my head and order me to do things. I was under the influence and control of demons and I needed a way out. Desperately, I prayed to God: "This isn't right, what can I do!?" Soon after this, on Good Friday, I had a vision of Jesus in my garden and He told me to take all the demonic books and have them burned; I had recurring visions of burning them. In the past I had almost given my life to Jesus in a church but ran away at the last moment. But now, I knew it was time. Two days later, on Easter Day, I took all my books to the nearest church and told the Pastor, "I've got a bit of a problem. I've got loads of books and I need to get rid of them." The Pastor asked me, "Are you ready to give your life to Jesus?" I said "Yes, yes, yes!" I handed him all the books on witchcraft, satanism and voodoo and he burned them in the incinerator. I asked Jesus to come into my life and one week later I was baptized in the sea off the North Wales coast, near my home.

Then Jesus spoke to me. His voice was different to the demonic voices I had been hearing. He was full of love and I felt peace and clarity when He spoke. He told me to find God TV, so I did and I came across a program called 'It's Supernatural' with Sid Roth. I was thinking how interesting the show was, and then Jesus' voice said, "Go onto your iPad and scroll back." I was looking for someone, but I didn't know who. It was then that I saw the program with Aliss. I watched it and I thought, "Oh my God, this woman's amazing!" and I realized that I'd love to be like her. She was talking about Jesus and her relationship with the Holy Spirit and she seemed to move in power unlike anything I'd come across before. But it was a pure power, full of God's love. She seemed happy and I knew I needed a relationship with God like she had.

I searched for her books and I bought all of them. I read them and kept reading all of them, I couldn't get enough. That was when I started really connecting to Jesus. I also booked myself onto a conference which Rob and Aliss were organizing in Chester, not far from my home in North Wales.

The following month, I attended the conference in Chester alone. No-one knew me, but as Aliss stood at the front of the meeting, I felt Jesus come up to me in a huge bright white light. Looking straight at me, Aliss called out, "There's somebody here who's just given their life to Jesus and has been reading my books." I was absolutely gobsmacked when she said that, but I went up onto the stage and shared some of my story with her in front of hundreds of people in the audience. Aliss then asked if I would like to be immersed in the Holy Spirit and I readily agreed, so everyone there stretched out their hands and began to pray over me as I went back to my seat.

I was aware of an incredible figure in front of me. It was Jesus and He was wearing robes that were so white and emanated a brilliant white light. He began to pull things out of the top of my head. I could feel demons being pulled out. I'd been in a lot of pain with my back and shoulders and throughout my body and then I realized I was totally and utterly pain free and I just felt amazing. After that, I felt the presence of Jesus so strong like He was standing right next to me and I could feel His robe brushing against me.

Following my encounter with Jesus at the conference, not only was I pain free, but I also no longer needed the antidepressant medication I had been taking. Up until the conference I practiced and taught Reiki, but afterwards discovered I could no longer do it. I gave up teaching it immediately; the Lord had totally removed it from me, and instead I was releasing the healing power of Jesus.

After a while, it seemed as though the presence of Jesus had faded away a little and I allowed some of my fears to return. I realized I needed to continue walking with Jesus every day and make daily choices. It was then that some pain began to come back into my body and I also had dreadful skin problems.

I wanted to get right with God, so I booked myself onto a workshop with Aliss and Rob. But when I arrived, I felt ill with back pain that continued into my arm and up into my head. I really felt awful and wondered how I was going to sit through the workshop as the pain seemed to get worse, but then thankfully, it was time for the practical. We got into twos and the person I was with told all the pain to leave me in the name of Jesus. I could feel all the pain go and I just felt amazing with no pain, no nothing. I told the demons to leave and they did, as soon as I broke any agreement with them, and my skin condition left too.

A few years ago, I changed my name to a demonic name, to try and get more power. But when I gave my life to Jesus, I knew I needed to get rid of that name, so I changed it back to the name I was given as a baby. It wasn't easy to change as all my friends were using my demonic name but doing that brought freedom too.

I know that the power of Jesus works. I can see it works. It has worked in my life. I know God is real. Jesus is the highest power, far greater than any demonic power. When I used to do Reiki, I would feel the Reiki symbols coming through me, they were being drawn through my body and out. I've not felt any of that since choosing to follow Jesus. What I feel now is pure; I'm tuning into a different energy totally and it's not Reiki, it's the power of Jesus, the Holy Spirit.

Following Jesus is incredible. The minute I battle against Him and the times I ignore God or go against Him is when the stress and the angst begin again, and then I feel myself opening up to a dark force. It's like a totally different mindset for me because I hadn't read the Bible before. It's all new to me. I said, "Lord Jesus I want to give you everything, I want to give you my life, I want to heal in your name. Use me as your instrument." And now He does. But I've still got a lot to learn. This is still all new to me, but I no longer feel powerless. As I lay down my life, He lives through me and He is so powerful.

The Lord has continued to guide and teach me. Things haven't always been easy, as the devil didn't want to let me go, but with the support of the church I attend and the support I am receiving from many wonderful Christians I am moving forward with the Lord. I've been able to use my testimony to help many others who are in the Occult and the New Age and other religions to know the truth and to turn to Jesus.

Going through the experience that I did has made it clear to me that the devil is real, that demons are real and they work through what we sometimes perceive as 'good', even 'white witchcraft'. We need to learn to discriminate and to understand and discern the difference. If you don't know Jesus, then absolutely make Him your friend, give your life to Him. When I think about some of the things I've been through in my life, I think He's always been there. I've had the opportunity to follow Jesus previously but each time I would walk away. Please DON'T walk away, just do it. It would have been better for me if I'd done it sooner, but I'm glad He didn't give up on me.

The Lord said to me, "I want you" and He's done many things to show me His love. I've not been a good girl, but it's amazing because He's chosen to forgive me for everything I've done wrong and He 'remembers it no more.' I don't even have to think about the bad stuff from my past as it's gone. I went through some dreadful things in my life, particularly with the stabbing, but the physical and emotional pain doesn't exist anymore: I'm free.

I pray for you as you read this, that you find the Lord Jesus and that you step into a new life, a new way of being. Take my example and change your life, please! One thing that concerns me is how easy it is to get hold of occult material and I would say if you're tempted please don't go down that route because demons are real and they will try and destroy you so don't do it. But if you have done that, it is not too late for you. You can have complete freedom through Jesus. Turn your life over to Him and get rid of any paraphernalia you may have from past sin. Have a good clear out and a fresh start with Jesus. You won't regret it.

Pray with Aliss:

"Heavenly Father, I choose to turn from my old ways to your ways. Help me not to want to take revenge or gain control or power over others. I ask you to forgive me for the times I have done that and I choose to forgive those who have hurt me. Father God, I repent and turn away from any involvement in occult practices, (name them: eg witchcraft, voodoo, satanism, paganism). Please forgive me by the blood of Jesus and set me free.

I choose to surrender my whole life to you. Please take over and give me a fresh start. Thank you that as a child of God I am a brand new person. The old has gone and the new is here! Amen."

Chapter Twelve
NEIL
Introducing Neil

A group of people had come to one of our workshops in Chester in order to be trained and activated to demonstrate the power of Jesus, and Neil was one of them. As Rob and I prophesied over Neil in the last session, we sensed that God was going to be working through him to impact many people, even though we knew nothing about him.

I was intrigued by Neil and wanted to find out more, especially when I discovered he had been one of the top snipers in the British Army! His story is powerful - let his miraculous transformation encourage you to ask God for your own miracle.

NEIL'S STORY

When I was born, I wasn't wanted. Instead, I was adopted into a large family. My early childhood wasn't too bad. I grew up in a nice little market town in England in the seventies. But my parents were strict. There were certain things I couldn't do, which caught the attention of the other boys at my school. I was often picked on, and my parents did little to help. So in a way, I was bullied at home, and I was bullied at school. There was no real let-up.

My safe place was in the nearby woods. I would go there with a friend, and mess about. I have no idea why, but there was always this blue nylon rope knocking around. We used to make swings: my friend would climb the tree, and I would be the one responsible for testing the swing out, and they were often very high up. Sometimes the rope wasn't strong enough, and I would pile into the river, the undergrowth or the brambles. One time, we found some steel cable, and an old milk crate, and we managed to make a 'death slide' right across the railway tracks. We used it again and again, until my friend got stuck at the highest point, a good twenty feet off the ground, and I had to catch him. We also went free climbing on cliffs near where I lived. We'd drop a rope down the face of the cliff from the top, and without any harness or safety gear, we'd clamber onto the rope and climb all the way down. We'd certainly have fallen to our deaths if we'd let go of the rope. We used to do stupid things, but we didn't care.

I was quite adventurous, and a bit mad. Even then, I wanted the adrenalin rush. My friend was also picked on at school, so we were good friends through that. He could relate to me so we got on well, and shared many adventures together. When we became teenagers, things changed slightly. We found out we could get served alcohol and the off-license (liquor store) would even serve us in our school uniforms. I thought nothing of having a drink in the morning, before school. Me and my friends knew there was always a chance of being caught, so we'd drink fast and then go out on the town causing trouble. Life was still difficult at home as well as at school, and this was my escape from all those feelings of anger, frustration, and loneliness.

Things that were quite insignificant by them-selves, eventually built up after days and days of the same emotional, verbal and physical abuse. I was told to ignore the bullies and that the bullying would eventually stop, but I remember asking, "When?" It started in my early teens and looking back, I can't remember a day when I wasn't abused. By the time I was sixteen-years-old, I could cope a little better with the beatings, and eventually I thought, "I'm not going to take this anymore. I'm not going to be someone's punch-bag all the time." So that's when I started fighting back. I read books and started kick-boxing. I was actually quite good and became a semi-professional kick-boxer. I could take more than a few punches, and it gave me a way to deal with the raw aggression that I had pent up inside. I could let it all out. When I first started, I would often get disqualified and had a reputation of being a bit of a 'beserker.'

Around this time I met Tina, the girl who would become my wife. Often I would sit in a tree by the river and get drunk. One such time, I'd been drinking and was sitting in the tree. Unfortunately, I lost my balance and fell out, right on top of Tina as she was walking along. I often tell people, instead of falling into the river that time, I fell in love!

Once I left school, I had many jobs, but got fired from almost every single one. I used to hit people or say things I shouldn't. Sometimes I'd decide I didn't want to do that job anymore and would just walk out. I had the control now, and I liked the fact I didn't have to do what I was told. I ended up in a few security jobs and became a bit of a vigilante at times. But if my boss asked me to do something I didn't want to do, I'd hit him and knock him out, and then go and get another job!

I also got involved in illegal street fighting around this time. I won some and lost some, but I escaped any bad injuries because I could take a beating. In a similar way, I taught myself to take emotional beatings. Anything that caused me pain or made me feel vulnerable, I shut out. I didn't feel much about anything. I loved my girlfriend Tina, but that was where it stopped.

Ever since I was a youngster, I'd dreamed of joining the army. I never applied though, because my parents were so against it. They would even sabotage my attempts by going to my careers' office and interfering. But after all my other jobs had fallen through I applied, and at the age of twenty-four, I was accepted. I knew I'd be sent abroad for training, so I called Tina right away and proposed over the phone. I asked if she wanted to come with me, and she did, so we got married. Tina was a believer, but I persuaded her to get married in a registry office. In many ways, our relationship was a negotiation. But she stuck by me, and she prayed for me all the time.

In infantry training, I was good. I had the fitness from kick-boxing and street-fighting. I was robust. I accepted the discipline because I knew I could never get another job elsewhere, so I stuck at it and gave it all I had. Most days I would run the seven miles to work and back. I went through physical training, I learned to handle a bayonet and rifles, and worked on the armored vehicles sometimes. Tina also worked on the barracks and after one year, we had our first child together. To be honest, life was good at that time. I soon won best at physical training, best combat infantryman and best shot. I discovered that on the firing range, in the two or three seconds that the targets flipped over, I could hit my target plus the targets in the lanes either side of me. If somebody was weak at shooting, they would go in the lane next to mine, give me spare ammunition and a little spare cash, and I would make them look good.

After one year, I was selected for sniper training. Snipers go out in pairs, to observe and report and, if necessary, take people out. It all relates to not being seen. After training, I was expected to get one-shot, one-kill, at six-hundred meters (or two-thousand feet). I found that I could actually hit targets with the same sight and the same rifle at up to a thousand meters, nearly double the requirement! For nine years between 1995 and 2004, I toured Bosnia, Northern Ireland, Kosovo, Iraq and Afghanistan. I scouted positions, I patrolled streets and I was shot at more than a few times. I witnessed many horrors: countless bombings where I've been thrown into the air by close explosions and I've been set on fire. It was extremely harrowing and I saw ethnic cleansing first-hand; piles of bodies at the roadside in Bosnia are etched into my memory.

I became attached to special forces, which tested my morals like nothing else. I was rarely afraid. Once, I was driving into town with a local soldier. He put his gun to my head and decided he was going to take me hostage. So I drove off the track and into a nearby minefield to scare him until he put the gun away. To be honest, most times I didn't value my life enough to be afraid.

In some places there would be illegal checkpoints and we'd have to fight just to get through them. Some checkpoints that had been abandoned along the roadside were like scenes from the second World War. A pile of luggage that had been rifled through, next to a pile of clothes and then further along I saw blood-stained earth with pieces of flesh and bone; the remains of people who had been shot and dumped in the nearby river.

I was in many life-and-death situations, but I never thought about God, or where I might go if I was killed. I didn't care about anything except the job at hand. I see now that God was there all along, protecting my life, despite my ignorance of Him.

The tours were tiring, and hardly good for family life. In 2005 I hurt my back a little and stepped away from most front-line activities. I started to drink more, really it was just to get to sleep and block out the memory of the awful things I had seen, or done. One such memory etched into my mind was of the time I awoke one night to find my comrade and friend, who was in the bed next to mine, with a rifle in his mouth. I was horrified, but before I had chance to do anything, I watched him pull the trigger. These horrific things were run-of-the-mill occurrences, and they piled up over the years, until I was signed off with a severe case of post-traumatic stress disorder. It also affected my short-term memory. I would get to the bar and forget what I'd gone to order. I would get up each morning and would have to ask my wife what to do next. I didn't know what I was doing from one minute to another. I had some counselling and was on medication, but I preferred a few beers and to put a mask over it all and pretend it wasn't there. I pretended I wasn't depressed, or drinking, or burned out in the way that I was.

Tina will tell people that back then, I was a very angry man. My life was surrounded by violence, and my instinct was to reach out with anger and violence. I was never violent to my wife or my sons, but if someone cut me up while driving, it was a different story. She will also tell people that I was lost. I would withdraw into myself a lot, and not let people reach me. Me and my family desperately needed something to change and one day, thankfully it did.

Tina had continued going to church throughout this time and one day was offered a family holiday at a church retreat center. I wasn't bothered, but she dragged me along with our two sons. I told her, "I'll go, but I ain't doing any of that Christian stuff – not a chance!" We had no money to go on a normal holiday as I drank most of it away, so we agreed to go on the church holiday as it was cheap.

I didn't want anything to do with religion, and as soon as we arrived at the retreat center, I hated it. It took her twenty minutes to get me out of the car and into the building. I did not want to be there. I kept thinking, "What am I doing here with these losers? These bearded, flip-flop-wearing do-gooders?" My attitude was poor. I would ignore people when they spoke to me, or I would dismiss them with a one-word answer or a disrespectful comment. I kept drinking, even though it was banned at the retreat. I would leave, head to the off-license, and drink on a park bench before going back. It got to one night, when I hated being there so much, that I entered a dark place and considered taking my life. I seriously thought about committing suicide on a church holiday. I had shame and guilt coursing through me, and I didn't want to talk to anybody about it, not even Tina.

Then one evening, I went for a walk and passed the little chapel where they held the services. A man who has since become a good friend of mine was by the door. He asked if I was coming in for the reflection service but I said, "No!" I told him that people like me don't do things like that. But he persuaded me, so I went inside. The reflection service consisted of a short Bible passage and a thought for the day. It was led by a vicar who was a little old woman. I can't remember her name, but I do remember she had the rare and amazing talent of carving a banana into the likeness of a pig!

She stood up and read from the gospel of Matthew, where Jesus tells all who are weary and burdened to come to Him, and He will give them rest. She gave us each a pebble to hold and told us to think of it as the burdens we wanted to be rid of. I sat there staring at my little pebble and sighed. I said to God, "If you really are there, then I need you now." When we were ready, we had to put our pebbles at the foot of a model cross. I don't know how long I sat there. It could have been ten seconds, but it felt like hours. I went to get up, and I couldn't lift the pebble. There I was, just out of the army, benching 200 kilos (440 pounds) and I could leg press 500 kilos at the gym, and I could not lift that pebble in my hand. I could really not lift it. It was everything I had carried around all my life, all my burdens, all the weight in my hands, in that little stone.

I finally managed to stand up with the thing. I must have looked ridiculous, because I was staggering, trying to carry it. I placed it at the foot of the cross. Then the weight dropped away, and I felt love. Real, unconditional love. It had always been there, on the fringes of my life, or inside little moments with Tina, but now I finally allowed it all to come in and it was the first time I'd been able to feel genuine love in my whole life. It's hard to put into words how I felt. I was awestruck. That night, I got into bed and fell asleep straight away. Tina still remembers how surprised she was to find me falling asleep without alcohol for the first time in years. I became a Christian – God really did save me, and for the first time in months, I knew what it meant to rest.

When I awoke the next morning, I was a different person. I no longer wanted to die and the depression was gone, just like that. There was no anger, no guilt, no shame. For the first time, I was interested in what was happening around me. People even said that I looked different. I still had post-traumatic stress disorder; there was still a journey to travel, with old temptations and emotions. But there was a different edge to it now. If I let God in to deal with those things, then He would heal me, and we could handle it. I had to choose to follow Jesus after all, and whenever I did, He always responded. That was the start of my new self. I went to church and everything I knew about life changed.

Now, a few years later, I'm the male leader for that same church holiday. We see out-and-out miracles every year. People just like me are finding God for themselves. Breaking free from financial, medical and family difficulties. They come back and share stories just like mine. I also travel to different countries, telling my story and speaking to people about Jesus. I tell them, "He is there for you, just as He was, and is, for me. You can have the same love, the same power, living in you." It's an honor to have those conversations. I've also spoken in front of 3,000 people including the Archbishop of Canterbury at Winchester Cathedral!

If you are reading this and you have had issues – anything from abuse or depression, to addictions, anger or suicidal thoughts – there is only one answer. His name is Jesus Christ and I am living proof that He is alive and that He works through anyone. He can transform you in a supernatural way and He can change your life for the better, even if you think He cannot accept you because you have done wrong. I couldn't have got any lower in my life. I knew I was a lying, thieving, cheating, murdering scum-bag. But all I had to do was to say sorry and invite Him into my life, and that is all you need to do too. You will be changed – it might not always be loud or dramatic, but it will be a starting point. Getting to know God is the best thing that ever happened to me. It's that starting point. He is there, and He will change your life beyond measure, without a shadow of a doubt.

Pray with Aliss:

"Father God, thank you that salvation through Jesus is the starting point into a whole new life, a whole new realm of the Kingdom of Heaven and a life in the Spirit. I pray that, just like a new-born baby has new life, that my new life through Jesus will grow and mature. Help me to do that. Put people around me that can help and encourage me to fulfill my destiny in you and that I will accomplish everything you have put me on this earth to do, through your love and power and for your glory, Amen."

Unexpected Miracles

Chapter Thirteen
YOUR STORY

Whether you have an obvious need in your life, or outwardly appear to be successful in every area, the truth is, we all need a miracle; we all need a Savior. Everyone has a void in their lives that only a relationship with Jesus can fill. We try and fill that void with things we think will make us happy. With Mark it was money, drugs and sex. With Sarah it was relationships, for Neil: alcohol and fighting. Lisa tried to fill the void with her career and spirituality. With Mandi it was drugs and for Kamran, religion. It could be any number of things, not always harmful: even fitness, family or charitable work. These things may fill the emptiness for a short time, but that void remains.

Each of these stories is different, but every person came to a point where they realized something was missing in their lives. Take Alex who had outward success – multilingual, CEO of an expanding business, beautiful fiancée - but he experienced a loneliness that nothing, not even his spiritual practices, were able to satisfy.

In addition to recognizing their need, each person then had to step out in faith and do something. In Sarah's case, she asked God to talk to her, but she also actively drove the thirteen miles to a restaurant where someone began to share about Jesus. Mark flew to Florida and then asked God to help him. He humbled himself by attending a prayer session and allowed himself to become so vulnerable that he filled out a booklet with all his sin for strangers and family members to read! Adrian shredded his tarot cards, Mandi surrendered to Jesus and removed herself from negative influences, Debra burned her demonic books and got baptized. Matt bought a Bible and shared his story in public, Lisa closed her business and gave up everything she knew. Kamran prayed to Jesus by faith even though he wasn't one-hundred percent sure, Alex gave up his home, his career and emigrated. Neil participated in a meeting he didn't want to be at, and Timothy saved up and went to a workshop.

As a result of admitting they had a need and then subsequently stepping out in faith, not knowing what would happen next, every one of these people experienced a dramatic transformation that could only have occurred through the grace and power of God. They each received an unexpected miracle which turned their lives upside down, or should I say, the right way up!

These biographies show that not none of these people were perfect. Mark even thought he was 'cooked and going to hell!' All of them, just like you and me, had made mistakes, but thankfully they weren't too proud to admit it. The Bible says that we "All have sinned and fallen short of the glory of God" (Romans 3:23), but Jesus paid the price and died for our sin. We can be forgiven, all our sins washed away through the blood of Jesus and when we come to Him, we are given a clean slate; a brand-new life through the resurrection power of Jesus. Don't make the mistake of thinking you can only come to God when your life is perfect. It will never happen!

The Bible says that Satan the thief comes to steal, kill and destroy (see John 10:10). One of the things the enemy is stealing in this day and age is people's identity; who you really are and who you were created to be. Kamran, Mark and Lisa recognized that they had lost their 'identity', but thankfully, our true identity can be found in Jesus Christ. When we enter into a personal relationship with Him, the Bible comes alive to us through His Holy Spirit, and we discover who God is and who we are in Him. Through knowing God and the truth of His Word, Mark, Kamran and Lisa each found their true identity. It's time to find yours.

Begin by talking to Jesus and tell Him how you're feeling. He cares about you. Be honest with yourself, with God and with those who care about you. Why not do what Mark did? Write down all the things you've been involved in, all the sin in your life; those things from the past that you're ashamed of, all the way through your childhood until the present day.

Include things that have been said or done to you that were bad, plus things you've said or done to others, past regrets and wrong motives.

Get it out into the open, into the light, and ask God to forgive you for those things. If you want some help, find someone you can trust – maybe a local church Pastor or a Christian friend. Ask them to pray for insight from the Holy Spirit and share anything they get with you. Then read out loud all the things you've written down. Confess your sin, turn away from it and God will forgive you. He will cleanse you from all your sin, through the powerful blood of Jesus and He will set you free. Ask Him to come into your life and fill you with His Holy Spirit.

As Sarah, Debra and Mandi discovered, when you ask Jesus to come into your life, you are born again and you become brand new, but the circumstances or the people around you may not change for the better. The demons in other people's lives around Sarah began to manifest and all sorts of things kicked off. She ended up going through some awful tragedies, but God looked after her and she kept trusting Him and now things are going well in her life. "We know that in all things God works for the good of those who love Him" (Romans 8:28). Even in the midst of chaos and tragedy, keep choosing to follow Him and allow Him to keep your heart soft, however tough the circumstances. "Follow the way of love and earnestly desire the things of the (Holy) Spirit" (1 Corinthians 14:1). As we begin to follow Jesus and meditate on the truths in the Bible, living them out each day, we will see new patterns emerging in our lives. The power of God can transform an empty lifestyle into one that is wholesome and fruitful.

Sometimes it isn't our own rebellion or wrong choices that have caused difficulties for us. Things that happen to us, through no apparent fault of our own can have a devastating effect on our lives. Take Neil and Mark who were both bullied at school. Mark had also been dedicated to the Masonic spirit which he wasn't even aware of. Sarah was the victim of abuse by others and Tim was electrocuted through somebody else's poor judgment. Many of us are the victims of other people's wrong choices or actions, however, we still need to choose to forgive those people, even if they are not sorry for the harm they caused us. Ask God to help you forgive every person He brings to mind who has wronged you. This is such a powerful thing to do and will bring you freedom and healing.

Most of us want to help others in some way. This was Lisa's motivation when she got drawn into New Age therapies. However, there's a verse in the Bible that explains how the god of this world has blinded people's minds from knowing the good news of Jesus (see 2 Corinthians 4:4). Adrian, Kamran, Lisa and Debra were all blinded from knowing the truth for some time. Maybe you've been blinded too, very subtly over the years, so you're not even aware of it. But since reading these stories, you're beginning to recognize that what you thought was the truth is not so certain anymore. What you thought was real power is just a sad substitute for the true love and power of the real Jesus, the Son of the Living God. The Bible warns us of another Jesus, a counterfeit Jesus, and as a result we can receive evil spirits instead of the Holy Spirit (see 2 Corinthians 11:3,4). A counterfeit Jesus is popular in New Age teaching and practices, but how wonderful that the counterfeit can be renounced so you can encounter the Truth: Jesus the Son of God Himself. The Bible says that when you know the Truth, the Truth will set you free.

Perhaps you have hit rock bottom like Sarah, Neil and Matt did, and are contemplating taking your own life or harming yourself in some way. Well, speak to those demons of suicide or self harm and tell them to stop tormenting you, in the name of Jesus. Know how loved you are by God. Often suicidal thoughts and self harm stem from rejection, so dig into the Word of God, the Bible, and just like Lisa did when she studied Ephesians, discover how precious you are to God. He has chosen you to be His child and, like Kamran discovered, His close friend. I pray for hope to rise up in your heart right now. That you will begin to see God's plan for your life. He has a good plan; not to harm you but for you to prosper – spirit, soul and body.

If someone close to you is living a destructive lifestyle or is in need of any sort of miracle, I want to encourage you that things can change. Prayer is powerful. Alex, Neil and Mark's wives constantly prayed for them. They may have been oblivious, but God always hears our prayers. And at just the right time, things can change so dramatically and so quickly that the miracle may come when you least expect it. The result of a praying family member or friend is powerful, or even in Matt's case, someone like me who didn't even know him but was provoked by the Holy Spirit to pray for him and his friend.

Why not give a copy of this book to someone you are praying for, so they can see there is hope and there is a way out, even when things seem impossible? God is good and He loves each one of us. He loves us so much that He sent His only Son to die in our place that we may be forgiven; that we may be made right and blameless through Jesus. Not only that, but through the power of His resurrection, enter into a life of love, joy and peace.

It has been a privilege for me to witness not only the amazing transformations in the lives of these people, but also to hear their life stories. It's clear that, even though the miracles seemed to happen suddenly, God's hand had been on their lives all along. He is a faithful God. Perhaps you could take some time to think back over your own life and see how God has intervened and how He has preserved your life and brought you this far.

My prayer for you, in the words of the Apostle Paul, is that through reading this book, your eyes are opened so you can see the difference between dark and light and choose light; that you would see the difference between Satan and God and choose God. I pray that you would accept God's offer of sins forgiven and a place in His family, and join the company of those who begin real living by believing and following Jesus (see Acts 26:17-18).

Some of the people you have read about in this book have their own websites. We have listed them, together with links on: **www.SpiritLifestyle.com**

Know someone who would
benefit from reading this book?

Order copies of

UNEXPECTED MIRACLES

www.SpiritLifestyle.com

We ship worldwide.

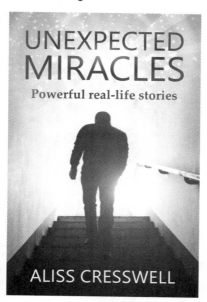

Plus:

The Believer's Guide to Survival

A great resource for new believers.